BOOK MARK

BOOK MARK

How To Be An Author

CHIP R. BELL
And Contributoring Authors

GEORGIA
WRITERS
MUSEUM
Every story
starts somewhere.

Eatonton, GA

For ordering information in special discounts for bulk purchases, please contact the Georgia Writers Museum in Eatonton, Georgia.

Image Credits Interior Stock Art From 123RF.com: Two Books with Glasses © marcin Marczak; Pencils and Doodles © hchjjl; Royalty Check © iqoncept; and, Cookbook © Igor Petrove.

Image Credits Interior Stock Art From Shutterstock.com: Calliope © Morphart Creation; Writers Block © Pixelbliss; Black Feather Pen © Anna Tyukhmeneva; Latin Letters in a Heap © Anton Balazh; Hand Drawn Book Case with Sleeping Cat © Franzi; Florishes © Pixel Embargo; Plan B @ Oksana Chemenko; This is My Story © Nokuro; Overturned Ink Bottle with Calligraphy © goldnetz; Newspaper Stack © Billion Photos; Book with Stars © NeMary; Feather Pen with seagulls © Blackspring; Helping Hands © hd connelly; Signature © PRILL; Best Seller © Artist_R.

Lyrics from "Being Green" by Joe Raposo, 1970, used with permission from the Disney Music Publishing.

Cataloguing-in-publication data

Bell, Chip R. and Contributing Authors

Book Mark: How to Be an Author / First edition, pages: illustrations; cm

ISBN: 978-0-692-06915-8

Cover art: Gail Vail
Book Cover and Interior Design: Ghislain Viau

Contents

Foreword

Legacy. It is what fuels teachers to be influential and coaches to be persuasive. It inspires authors and artists to treasure the reach and longevity of their artistic expression. Legally, a legacy is a bequest or gift handed down from the past, a historical perspective.

Legacy, however, is more than just history. It is also a concept that suggests that a person's contributions have been given special status.

The walls of the Georgia Writers Museum showcase the literary legacy of every author inducted into the Georgia Writers Hall of Fame with photos of renowned novelists like Margaret Mitchell, Pat Conroy, Alice Walker, Flannery O'Conner and Joel Chandler Harris. They include important social leaders like Dr. Martin Luther King, Jr., Dr. W.E.B. Du Bois, and President Jimmy Carter.

Their collective works form a legacy that inspires all writers with the potential that their own works could be an enduring and valued bequest...a legacy...to civilization.

As important as the celebration of the legacy of past Georgia authors, Georgia Writers Museum is dedicated to future authors who might someday earn that special status and have their photos on the wall.

The book you are holding is part of that special status-giving legacy, an opportunity to become an inductee into a rare and special group. Its ultimate goal is to equip its readers with the competence and confidence to kindle, nurture, and promote their literary talents.

The concept of *Book Mark* was spawned by a volunteer of Georgia Writers Museum as a special resource for writers eager to be authors. It includes chapter contributions of Georgia authors who have had their literary works published. Many have written award-winning books; some have achieved national and international best-selling prominence. All bring their depth of experience and wealth of expertise to this book.

We dedicate this book to the fledgling writers of Georgia, in the hopes it will inspire and instruct a legacy of literary excellence. May your words resound across Georgia while your message makes its "mark" across America and beyond. Surely one of you is destined for the Georgia Writers Hall of Fame.

> John P. Dennis, President
> Georgia Writers Museum
> Home of GA Writers Hall of Fame Exhibit

Prologue

Welcome, Writers

"There is no greater agony than bearing
an untold story inside you."
—Maya Angelou, *I Know Why the Caged Bird Sings*

"**I**'m an author" is one of the coolest answers to the question: "What do you do?" The label brings up visions in the minds of others of your midnight oil burning. It signals to them that you must be creative, talented, and highly disciplined. It says you are probably very knowledgeable about a particular subject, and/or you have an imagination the size of Texas. You are in the company of other authors like William Shakespeare, John Grisham, Alice Walker, and **Harry Potter** author, J.K. Rowling.

Being an author means you have completed a big writing project that is now out in public. But, before you are an author, you are a writer. There are millions of writers; there are fewer published authors. And, there are much fewer published authors who exercised a writing yardstick that measures them as a "good author." The goal of this book is to help you get from "being a writer" to "being a good author." At a deeper level, it is a way for you to use your book to make a mark on the lives of others—a book mark.

We created this special book for you because we have all been precisely where you are today. We have all traveled on that joyful (and sometimes painful) journey from writer to author. Our hope is this book will make your expedition one that is exhilarating, fun, and potentially profitable. Be forewarned. We cannot remove all the anxiety from your writer-to-author trip. Just as all great roller coaster rides have their happy squeals, they also have their scary moments that can make your heart race. Writing a book is a lot like a roller coaster ride. So, fasten your seatbelt!

We have assembled a book that covers most of the major parts of book authoring—from a rough idea to a royalty check! There are many more resources available to you. We have included some in the resources section at the end of this book. Since we are associated with the Georgia Writers Museum, we can also provide you connections to people who can help you continue your exciting journey.

Now, sit back in your favorite spot for reading and get ready for your thrilling ride toward "becoming an author."

Chapter 1

Preparing You
To Be an Author

"I'm writing a book. I've got the page numbers done."

—Steven Wright

Kermit the Frog sang a powerful song in "The Muppet Movie!" Part of the lyrics capture the joys and woes of being a writer. First, the opening lyrics written by Joe Raposo:

> *"It's not easy being green. It seems you blend in with so many other ordinary things. And people tend to pass you over 'cause you're not standing out like flashy sparkles in the water or stars in the sky."*[1]

Being a writer means staring at a note pad or computer screen wondering when inspiration will finally appear. It is a deep and longing search for flashy sparkles and stars to guide your way. It means late nights working and long days waiting to learn if your book has been accepted by a literary agent or publisher. Ernest Hemingway nailed the agony when he said, "There is nothing to writing. All you do is sit down at a typewriter and bleed!"[2] Mark Twain was a bit more upbeat in his assessment, "Writing is easy. You just remove the words that don't fit."[3] It means worrying about cover design and grammar and proofreading again and endorsements and reviews and book sales. And, so many other ordinary things.

But, there is another side. Kermit's song changes to a brighter melody, just like writing.

"But green's the color of Spring. And green can be cool and friendly-like. And green can be big like the ocean, or important like a mountain, or tall like a tree."

Being a writer can mean connecting with a magical spirit that fills your soul with abundant joy. It means riding the roller coaster of inspiration when it finally starts flowing with you. It means reading your work aloud to connect with the sounds, not just the words. It means reading back over your work and marveling at the result you seem to have mysteriously crafted. It means holding the first copy with an elation similar to holding a newborn baby you helped birth. It is a deep sense of satisfaction that you have accomplished a difficult feat while contributing to your readers' inspiration, enjoyment, education, and improvement.

Few vocations or avocations are as public as the output of an author. Where is the signature in the court case lawyers win, the malady doctors arrest, or the tax return accountants prepare? But, a book has your very personal moniker on its cover. It pronounces to all the world—on the front and on the spine, the identity of its creator. It is why some writers are perceived as having healthy egos or oversized pride. They are safeguarding not just their unique work, but their very individuality.

Being an author is a way to put a piece of you into the universe that can make its mark on others for a very long time. It is a format that can influence far beyond your daily contact and interactions with others. And, it can leave behind a legacy that says you were here on this planet and you made a difference.

Kermit ends: "I am green and I'll do fine, it's beautiful! And, I think it's what I want to be."

And, maybe your response to this book will be: "Let me be a writer. I think it's what I want to be!"

Chapter 2

The Critical Success Factors of Authoring

"It does not do to leave a live dragon out of your calculations, if you live near him."

—J.R.R. Tolkien, *The Hobbit*

Warning. This is the toughest chapter in this book! There is a very practical reason for covering this topic early. Before writing a book, it is important to take a clear-eyed, sober assessment of your capability to write your book and your target market's ability to buy it (marketability).

Let's be clear. Authors write books for many reasons. Some people just want bragging rights. The fact that their book is self-published and read only by a handful of people is just fine; they can technically say, "I'm an author." Some want to add "author" to their calling card or resume. Some view their book as a giveaway to help a charity or cause. These are all legitimate reasons to write a book. But, if any of these reflect your goal, best of luck. You can skip this chapter as well as Chapter 16 on marketing your book. But, if you are interested in selling lots of copies of your book, what follows are a few key factors to consider.

The SWOT of Authoring

For several years, Mary and Tom Jones enjoyed having friends over for dinner. While doing a year's graduate study in Italy, Mary had learned to make superb pizza. Tom prided himself on having an enormous knowledge of wines. After Mary's high school teaching position was cut during a budget squeeze, she and Tom decided to put their savings into a classy wine and pizza shop. Mary could supervise the cooking; Tom could buy the wine and handle the business management while continuing a moderately demanding job as an electrical engineer.

They leased space in a new inner-city shopping mall and began their new career as restaurateurs. Within six months, they were out of business! Mary learned she lacked the patience and desire to supervise people. Tom had been unable to keep up with the continual paperwork. Even worse, the mall generated mainly lunch traffic; less than 25 percent of their business came from dinner customers. The waiting time for their specialty, made-to-order pizza, precluded the rapid customer turnover required to capitalize on the lunch business. They went into bankruptcy, bitterly resigned, exhausted.

You may be saying, I would never make that kind of mistake. Perhaps not. But, there are many potholes you can easily trip on unless you objectively assess and plan your book strategy. In the world of strategic planning, the process is called SWOT—strengths, weaknesses, opportunities, and threats. And even the most creative, forward-thinking author has stepped in a hole because he or she failed to do a thorough SWOT.

Strengths of Your Book Strategy

Strengths are assets that set you apart from others. Strengths come in many forms. They can be features of your reputation, resources you can uniquely access, or a special knowledge of your subject. They can be powerful advocates who can lobby the marketplace on behalf of your book. Keep in mind, you are cataloging those strengths that will help you decide if serious authoring is right for you. It is not enough to craft a book; it is bringing that book to the public arena and making it a good seller that really counts. Use the questions below to start your thinking. Then, invite others to build on your list. Your friends can give you a reality check on what you consider your strengths. Be prepared to remove some of the items you initially thought were strengths.

- Is your reason for writing this book anchored to your passion?
- Would others consider you a very good writer?
- Are you willing to make personal sacrifices for this book?
- Are you writing this book to please your readers (Or, is it mostly about just satisfying you?)

- Do you have deep knowledge of the subject of your book? How about your target market (the anticipated buyers of your book)?
- Do you have the time, energy, experience, and resources to effectively complete this book and bring it to the market?
- Is this your first book? If yes, do you have access to expert helpers?

Weaknesses of Your Book Strategy

A weakness is a limitation, shortcoming, or restriction that you can or cannot control. This part of your SWOT analysis is not about listing your imperfections as much as it is getting an up-close and personal view of the drawbacks that might make your book strategy flawed. Some people assume cataloging weaknesses is completely different from listing strengths. It sometimes is. But often the most useful approach is to look at the dark side of your strengths. Your greatest strength can be your biggest blind spot. Answer the questions below and then review them with your SWOT advisors.

- Are you defensive when receiving feedback, especially if your view is different?
- Do you expect to achieve some measure of fame and/or fortune by writing this book?
- In the past has writing been an activity for which you needed something exterior to keep you on task? A deadline, another person, personal guilt?
- Is this book really just a hobby to keep you busy? Is it about your legacy?

- Are you a bit uncertain about whether you have the capacity to go the distance and finish?
- Can you name and describe the top ten books in your book genre that are likely to be your book's main competitors?
- Is your book a really cool idea and nothing more at this point?

Opportunities for Your Book Strategy

Opportunities are openings for success. Opportunities come in many forms. They can range from a sudden trend, popular fad, or hot topic you happen to know a lot about. Opportunities could be created by other events that leave you with an edge. They can be as serendipitous as a diary a distant relative left you that contained a compelling story waiting to be told. They can be a hole in your book market where there is pent-up demand but little content. Answer the questions below and then get feedback from others.

- Are there zero (or very few) books in your target market similar to the one you plan to write?
- Have books similar to yours fallen short of their stated marketplace goal?
- Has a new market niche emerged (or is emerging) that would want to buy your book?
- If one percent of your target market bought your book, would it be deemed a success? How about one tenth of one percent?

- Do you possess an asset or talent you would consider unique or rare that could be used to write this book and make it a success?
- If you were a book publisher, would you pay a large advance for your book?
- Do you have access to information, stories, people, records, etc. that would be valuable content for your book?

Threats to Your Book Strategy

A threat is anything that could hamper or trip up your book strategy. It could be an economic hiccup, like a new book related to the technology world right before the dot com industry crashed. Competitor actions often constitute threats. Threats could be oversaturation in the marketplace by similar books. Threats could be the aftermath of negative publicity related to your subject. Getting thin, lowering cholesterol, or being politically edgy have all created winners and losers.

- Is there any likelihood a competing author could scoop your book strategy and preempt your launch, leaving you having to abandon your book project or risk looking like "me too"?
- Is the target market for your book declining in size? Are they buying fewer books?
- If every book sold was due to your direct effort, would your book fail to become financially viable?
- Are there generational shifts that could adversely impact your target market?
- Have you thought mostly about the consequences of a successful book (while not considering the opposite)?

- Are there negative, dark historical issues in society that your new book could inadvertently resurrect or invigorate?
- Have you considered today's overall decline of traditional books and bookstores?

The "Yes" answers to the 28 questions should point to areas of promise and areas of hazard. Again, a "jury of your peers" will be an asset in bringing objectivity to what is clearly an emotional endeavor. Keep in mind an important reality: unless you are a celebrated author with a track record of writing major best-sellers, publishers today don't sell books. They produce and print books and leave the selling to you.

Beyond "Setting Target Dates"

Inclusion is always a powerful book-marketing principle. Who are the important voices in your marketplace? Start growing and expanding your network. It will be crucial to launching your new book. Pay close attention to the chapter called "With a Little Help from Friends." Before finalizing your decision to write a new book, why not run it up the flagpole of your advisors as well as a few future book buyers in your genre and niche market? Passing their early snicker test could save you great expense now and embarrassment down the road.

The *New Yorker Magazine* ran a clever cartoon in the early eighties that portrayed an obviously well-to-do businessman reading his newspaper while sitting on a park bench. Beside him sat a dingy street bum. The businessman's reading is interrupted with the bum providing the caption under the cartoon: "You know where I think I went wrong? I never set target dates!"[4] The cartoon captures the core of the challenge. Strategy planning is important to success. However, execution requires more than "setting target dates." What follows are ways to turn an idea and plan into execution.

Chapter 3
Inviting Inspiration to Join Your Writing

"Write about what you know and care deeply about. When one puts one's self on paper—that is what is called good writing."
—Joel Chandler Harris

Muse. It is a word you will likely hear a lot as a writer. The word rhymes with "fuse"—as in the string used to light a firecracker. In some ways, the concept of a muse has a very similar meaning to the definition of a fuse! You will hear the word used in its singular form and sometimes in its plural form as in "the muses." Here is the backstory on the word.

In both Greek and Roman mythology, "The Muses" were the nine daughters of Zeus and Mnemosyne. Zeus was the head dude of everything and ruled the universe from Mount Olympus. The Muses were the goddesses of inspiration in literature, science, and the arts. Each presided over a different art form. For example, Terpsichore was over dance, Erato was over love poetry, and Calliope (pictured above) was over epic poetry, etc. Their role was to inspire ingenuity and creativity—something for which every writer longs. William Shakespeare wrote, "Oh! for a muse of fire, that would ascend the brightest heaven of invention."[5]

Your muse could be a personification of your concept of God, the Holy Spirit, or your dear grandmother who passed away. While it is a spiritual concept, it is not necessarily a religious one. The form of your muse is less important than accessing the powerful voice and inspirational spirit of your muse. Writers describe its presence as an unmistakable, mysterious feeling of encouragement, creativeness, and joy. Some characterize its potent influence as being the sole source of what ends up on their written page. Literary giant Norman Mailer called it "the spooky art." One writer we know told us, "I felt like I was just taking dictation from a higher power—something blessed and given to me as a gift."

Writers can get right misty-eyed when speaking of their muse. As mysterious as it all might sound, it can be a practical resource for your creative productivity, lighting the fuse to your imagination. It can be a cherished friend that leaves you deeply moved and warmly delighted when it appears. How do you get in touch with this magical, mystical spirit and harness its special power? Here are a few ideas.

Use a Creative Crossover

Most people have some creative outlet. It might be repairing cars, baking, sewing, playing an instrument, or even feeling a crappie hit a lure under a lake dock. It is an endeavor that uses your resourceful instinct, not your reasonable logic. Since "the muses" work across all creative outlets, finding inspiration in one arena can alert you of their presence, signaling you to go get your writing pad or turn on your computer.

Open your mind (and heart) to that sensation when a creative act seems to flow with amazing ease. Be patient and listen to its playful side. Take a walk with the goal of noticing artistic details around you—a flower, the sound of children at play, a bird, or the colors in the sky. Follow its current back to you, not you to the object, sound or color. Relax and quiet your mind. Ancient sages called it the state of "no mind" since you are letting creativity in, not seeking it out. You are not thinking; you are just being and noticing.

Believe in the Power of Your Muse

In his poem "What If You Slept," Samuel Taylor Coleridge speaks to the challenge of believing in mystery and magical moments. The poem reads,

"What if you slept.
And what if in your sleep,
you dreamed.
And what if in your dream

15

you went to heaven,
and there plucked a strange and beautiful flower.
And what if when you awoke you had that flower
   in your hand?
Ah, what then?"[6]

Muses can be shy and reserved. They appear where there is acceptance and openness. They stay away when there is an atmosphere of criticism and judgment. Muses are playful. When you "play" with your writing, they feel welcomed. They are kin to goodness. The more there is a wholesomeness in your effort, the more likely they will join you in it. "Do not hoard what seems good for a later place in the book, or for another book; give it, give it all, give it now," wrote writer Annie Dillard.[7] The advice is in part about setting a hosted table of purity for your muse.

This might sound like a bunch of hocus pocus to the rational, logical side of you. You might be wanting to put it in the same category with ghosts, fairies, and unicorns. But, your spiritual, inventive side recognizes it to be true. Trust your instinct; ignore your reason. At least for now! Ernest Hemingway is often quoted as saying, "Write drunk; edit sober." If he actually said it, he was being rather literal; what we mean is to write unbridled and without inhibition, and to edit objectively with accuracy and precision.

Invite Your Muse

Carry a scratch pad, note cards, or writing journal with you pretty much everywhere. When a phrase or example or idea hits you, write it down. The fact that it is "partially baked" is unimportant. It is a signal to your muse that you are working and serious about what you are doing. Some writers find having a special place or setting for their creative work helps free their mind and open their heart. Some listen to music and let the sounds and harmony become part of their muse invitation. But, the main message is this: do not multi-task; it is rude to your muse. Either write or don't write; never half-write!

Do not sit and wait for your muse to show up. Start writing… anything, silly stuff, sentences you would never share with anyone. Think of it like a duck hunter's call. But, instead of trying to attract ducks, you are welcoming your muse. Renowned poet Maya Angelou wrote, "What I try to do is write. I may write for two weeks 'the cat sat on the mat, that is that, not a rat.' And it might be just the most boring and awful stuff. But I try. When I'm writing, I write. And then it's as if the muse is convinced that I'm serious and says, 'Okay. Okay. I'll come.'"[8]

Talk with a Child

Young children have fewer learned mental governors than most adults. They approach life with a more curious, lighthearted perspective than adults, who can be steeped in rules, restrictions, and responsibilities. Ask the child of a friend or a relative to talk with you about your book idea. Describe your vision of a plot, theme, or main message and then listen to the child's reaction. Put on your most adventuresome hat and approach this significant conversation with a learning goal, not a validation goal. Accept what the child tells you as a relevant piece of a puzzle. It is not important now to know where it fits, just that you are able to be entertained and freed to be inspired.

Just Let Go

If you scramble the two words "Let Go," you get LT. Ego! And, "Lieutenant Ego" is only interested in "rightness," not "wonderfulness." Your LT. Ego has lots of self-defeating messages for you at the time you attempt to free-associate and write creatively. LT. Ego has zero interest in your self-esteem, only in the need to be perfect. Some messages might include, "This blank screen is a not-so-subtle message," "My English teacher was right," "I need to sound smart," "I don't have anything original to say," "I am masquerading as a writer," or "Tomorrow." Value your strict lieutenant, but let it know it is not needed right now. At this moment, you are a receptacle of brilliance and ingenuity. And, your creative side wants you to fall in love with that part of you! Embrace your greatness; value your uniqueness. Be your best friend!

Follow Its Discipline, Not Yours

When your muse visits it can offer you far more than you can use. Writers speak of wishing its insights had come much more slowly so they could have written or typed more of it. Painters speak of mental images they are trying to capture on canvas but soon realize that, like recalling a dream, there is more than can be remembered. Their experiences suggest following the flow of the muse, not trying to coach or direct it. It means getting up in the middle of the night when it awakens you with an idea and not promising to remember it the following morning and just going back to sleep. It means accepting that if it stops before you know it has finished, you have likely taken control. Redouble your invitation for its return and make a commitment to be less domineering.

Respect Its Power

Carlos Santana is one of the greatest guitarists who has ever lived. Following an amazing concert in Panama as he relaxed backstage, he was asked by a fan with a backstage pass, "How do you play the guitar so effortlessly?" His answer was a muse-inspired answer. "I do not play the guitar; the guitar plays me!" It was an expression of respect for the work he did and the instrument that enabled it. Treat your writing that same way. Don't take yourself seriously; take your work seriously. Prime the creative pump by starting and stopping at a happy place. Ernest Hemingway put it this way: "You write until you come to a place where you still have your juice and know what will happen next and you stop and try to live through until the next day when you hit it again."[9] Author George Heiring suggests writing one sentence at the new starting place before stopping in order to provide a jump start for the next day's writing adventure.

"At its best, the sensation of writing is that of any unmerited grace," wrote Annie Dillard. "It is handed to you, but only if you look for it. You search, you break your heart, your back, your brain, and then—and only then—it is handed to you."[10] Inspiration is to writing what heat is to cooking or fuel is to an engine. Without it, writing reads like an instruction manual or a telephone book. Inspiration is as free as air; it is also as priceless. Inspiration is available to everyone, especially someone like you with an interest in writing something of value. You are its great friend. Welcome it, nurture it, celebrate it, and it will visit you often.

Chapter 4
Unblocking
Writer's Block

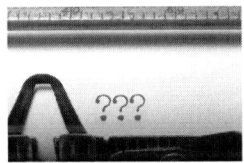

*"I do not over-intellectualize the production process.
I try to keep it simple: Tell the damned story."*
—Tom Clancy

There is a good writer inside most of us! Now, we know many people don't look in the mirror and see a writer staring back. When the topic of writing comes up, some folks are quick to say, "I'm just not creative," "I don't have anything important to say" or "I have no idea where to start." And, when they start to write, there remains a blank page for way too long. It is like the creative juices get plugged up in the pipe between the mind and pen. Curing writer's block is not about something you start doing; it is about something you *stop* doing.

What is writer's block? It is a writer's version of "Uh…" It can feel like a brain freeze or a mental blank screen. You are looking for a word or theme or idea and absolutely nothing seems to be surfacing in your mind. It can feel like seeing someone at a party you are supposed to know but you cannot recall that person's name. And, it is a worrisome barrier to bountiful writing.

All beginning writers get blocks! Here is how English novelist Phil Pullman put it:

"Writer's block…a lot of howling nonsense would be avoided if, in every sentence containing the word *writer,* that word was taken out and the word *plumber* substituted; and the result examined for the sense it makes. Do plumbers get plumber's block? What would you think of a plumber who used that as an excuse not to do any work that day?

"The fact is that writing is hard work, and sometimes you don't want to do it, and you can't think of what to write next, and you're fed up with the whole damn business. Do you think plumbers don't feel like that about their work from time to time? Of course, there will be days when the stuff is not flowing freely. What you do then is *make it up.* I like the reply of the composer Shostakovich to a student who complained that he couldn't find a theme for his second movement. 'Never mind the theme! Just write the movement!' he said."[11]

Pullman is not denying the existence of writer's block; he is arguing for a different approach to unblocking that pipeline between hidden wisdom and obvious words. Finding the best approach is a very personal one, but below are a few tips you can use to concoct your own antidote to writing stuck-ness!

Be Kind to Your Inner Writer

Avoid giving yourself negative messages, the ones filled with disapproval. Tell yourself, "I am a good writer" and start acting on that message. "Fake it til you make it" is not about a falsehood but rather about you talking to that good writer inside you looking for the exit door. Superstar tennis player Venus Williams said, "You have to believe in yourself when no one else does. That makes you a winner right there."[12] Positive self-talk is what great artists, athletes, and performers do to get in their "spirit of greatness." By using positive self-talk, you are doing two things—creating a pleasant landing pad for your muse and preparing your subconscious mind to help out.

Scientists have long believed the subconscious mind cannot differentiate between a real experience and an imagined one. That is why dreams can be nightmares. Famous golfers walk the golf course in advance of a championship match, playing each hole perfectly in their minds. Use personal pep talks to encourage your creative mind to get ready for sparkly imagination and adventuresome stories. When you write, surround yourself with fun, happy, supportive objects, scenes, people, and sounds.

Write Through the Block

When your vehicle suddenly drops off the highway, you know that jerking it back on the pavement is not wise, rather you must gradually guide it back on. Getting up and walking around, or leaving it for later is like jerking a car back onto the highway. It might make you feel calmer, but it can do little to correct the block. When you return to your work, you are likely to still be blocked. Blocks can occur when you are forcing and controlling your muse instead of working with it.

When you get a case of writer's block, keep writing...anything. Great athletes play through their pain. The same is true for writers. Write through your block. Rewrite an early chapter as a way to prime the creative pump. The great novelist John Steinbeck said, "Pretend that you're writing, not to your editor or to an audience or to a readership, but to someone close, like your sister, or your mother, or someone that you like."[13]

Or, Take a Break

Now, this is in complete contrast to the advice in the previous section. When you are dealing with a creative art form like writing, approaches and methods need to be personal, tailored to what works for you.

Clear your head. Engage in an activity very different from writing...a long walk, a shower, listen to music, cook something. Some writers suggest not talking with other people during your mental break. When you return to your writing, give yourself more encouraging messages. Avoid forcing thoughts...just let thoughts come to you.

Novelist Orson Scott Card wrote, "Writer's block is my unconscious mind telling me that something I've just written is either unbelievable or unimportant to me, and I solve it by going back and reinventing some part of what I've already written so that when I write it again, it is believable and interesting to me. Then, I can go on. Writer's block is never solved by forcing oneself to "write through it," because you haven't solved the problem that caused your unconscious mind to rebel against the story, so it still won't work for you or for the reader."[14]

Take the Eraser Off Your "Writing Pencil"

This means turning your "grammer teacher" button off. Stop writing with a governor on. You know what a governor does to a vehicle; it limits how fast it can go. A writing governor reminds you about grammar, punctuation, and editing. Those are important tasks to save for later, not when you are in the middle of being creative. Famous author Ernest Hemingway wrote, "Don't write holding your pencil too tight! Just let go and have fun."[15]

Now, notice how badly you wanted to change misspelled "grammer" to "grammar" in the first sentence. It is a metaphor. Stop thinking about syntax, split infinitives, dangling participles...or even misspelled words. Edit functions interrupt the flow of your imaginative work. The editing process abruptly shifts your mind to its left side, where reason resides, and away from the right side where creativity lives. The right side of your brain processes information holistically, artistically and without the pursuit of concrete patterns; the left side processes it rationally, logically, as it looks for concrete patterns. Want proof? Examine the figure below. The answer is at the end of the next chapter.

Count Every Square You See

Stop Gorging and Start Nibbling

Avoid trying to "eat the elephant with a single bite." Start with short, easy writing tasks as you build your writing confidence. Select positive, encouraging friends to give you feedback. Practice, practice, practice. Make writing an adventurous treasure hunt and be ready to learn as you go. Be proud of each step and celebrate your success. One writer frequently writes short 250-300-word blogs for his website. These blogs turn into 1,000-word articles he sends to magazines. At some point, they become the chapters in the writer's book. The point is, writing a whole book can be overwhelming. But, writing a short story or a short blog is not so daunting. Poet Alice Friman writes that to be a poetry book writer, you need to write a lot of poems. Approach your work by nibbling on a piece, not gorging on the whole project.

Court Your Book in Progress

Assume your book is a lover you are courting. You would treat it with the utmost of kindness and attention. You would tell your best friends all about it. You would bring it colorful and delectable gifts. A book in progress needs your affection, not your distain when it becomes difficult. Stake yourself out by telling others about the awesome book you are writing. UK prime minister Benjamin Disraeli wrote, "The author who speaks about his books is almost as bad as a mother who talks about her own children."[16] Write down clever thoughts, cool quotes, unique phrases, simple stories and then read them to your book in progress like a gift. When you start loving your book, it will start loving you back.

Writer's block is not like a ravine you cannot drive over; it is more like a log along your creative path that you need to get beyond. It comes for many reasons, sometimes for reasons you will never understand. Instead of focusing on why blocks come, spend time on how to get on the other side. Like imaginary friends who refuse to talk with you, treat writer's blocks with kindness, but determination. And, promise yourself they will not deter you from your goal of becoming an author.

Chapter 5

The Writer's Workout

"I get a lot of letters from people. They say: '
I want to be a writer. What should I do?' I tell them
to stop writing to me and get on with it."

— Ruth Rendell

Discipline. It is a word that gets very mixed reviews. When applied to raising children, it is generally viewed positively, but when applied to getting rid of that midriff bulge, not so much. All professions have disciplines, even those that involve creative expression.

Great writers use a discipline to keep their creative energy active. Some write at a particular hour; some write a set number of words each day. Like any vocation or avocation, the more you do it, the better you get at it. And, betterment means inspiration comes faster, flow occurs more easily, and blocks come less frequently.

"A simple rule," wrote playwright Norman Mailer. "If you tell yourself you are going to be at your desk tomorrow, you are by that declaration asking your unconscious to prepare the material. You are, in effect, contracting to pick up such valuables at a given time. Count on me, you are saying to a few forces below: I will be there to write."[17] Renowned fiction writer Terry Kay says, "Writing is easy when you are merely a typist. Good writing is very hard. And, it only starts with your third completely new draft."[18]

Keep the Writer in You Always Turned On

In the hit movie **The Magic of Belle Isle**, washed up, famed Western novelist Monte Wildhorn (played by Morgan Freeman) is coaching his 10-year-old neighbor Finnegan O'Neil to be a writer. She is having a difficult time with the concept of imagination. "Imagination," Monte tells her, "is the most powerful force ever made available to mankind." Once she finally understands the concept of seeing with her mind's eye, he tells her to, "Never stop looking for what's not there."[19] It is a vital part of a writer's discipline.

Need an example? Let's say you were having breakfast with a famous newspaper cartoonist and you are curious about how he works with imagination. Your conversation might go something like this:

"So, how do you come up with cartoon ideas?" you ask. Your cartoonist friend answers, "The cool ideas are everywhere. I just pick something and daydream about what it might be like. You have to let it work you as much as you making it work."

You probe a bit deeper: "Can you give me an example?"

"Well, give me a subject, any subject, and let me see where it wants me to take it," the cartoonist suggests. You are struck by how he speaks of ideas as if they were good friends with a mind of their own. Let's assume a man was at that very moment walking by the street-side window with a French poodle on a leash. So, you suggest, "How about a cartoon about a dog?"

The cartoonist says, "Why don't we put the dog in a restaurant like this one having breakfast with his new owner." As he begins to draw on his large sketch pad, the woman at the table nearby orders a cappuccino. "Aha," says the cartoonist, "Let's have the dog drinking a cappuccino!" And with that, his drawing pen portrays the dog with lots of steamed-milk foam on his mouth.

With a wide-eyed look of satisfaction, he exclaims, "Done! All we need is a caption; I think I have just the one!" He pencils in the lines the dog in the cartoon is speaking to his owner seated across from him at a restaurant table.

"My last owner wouldn't let me order this, said it made me look crazy!"

You laugh! But your quest for symmetry might force you to continue: "But, why not have the caption say, 'said it made me look mad?'" The cartoonist smiles and answers: "The creative part of humor is to let the viewer fill in the pattern. There would be little to 'get' if you made it totally obvious. It needs to pop in the viewer's mind like the punch line of a joke." Again, like the cartoonist, always stay on the lookout for what's not there. Create a word pattern that invites the reader to complete the image through insight.

Fall in Love with the Tools of Your Craft

Every craft relies on its tools. Painters depend on the quality of the paint that goes on the canvas and the type of hair used in the brush they use to put is there. Your primary tool is the word. Words are not the real thing any more than the image the painter displays on the canvas. The word "butterfly" is not a butterfly. Words are language fabrications that evoke mental images in the mind of the reader. "Words mean. Words point," wrote author Susan Sontag, "They are arrows. Arrows stuck in the rough side of reality."[20] Loving the tools of your artistry suggests taking great care to select the precise word that best captures the imagery in your mind that you intend will "copy and paste" in the mind of your reader. Respect the power of words as tools of understanding. Select them with meticulous care. Display them properly, always honoring the rules of grammar that govern their proper presentation.

Only the Good Stuff Survives

After the creative part comes the editing part. Cutting out words, phrases or paragraphs you deem mediocre or just okay can be tough. But, it is one of the most important parts of being an effective author. Think of it like this: if you were a renowned creative writing teacher and one of your students turned in the words and phrases in question, how would the words and phrases be evaluated? Only the very best should survive. This is not a quest for word count or book completion; it is the pursuit of excellence. This book not only has your name on the cover; it has your signature on every page.

Annie Dillard, in her book **The Writing Life** put it this way: "How many books do we read from which the writer lacked courage to tie off the umbilical cord? How many gifts do we open from which the writer neglected to remove the price tag? Is it pertinent, is it courteous, for us to learn what it cost the writer personally?"[22]

Proof read your final work many times. When you proof read, be sure to read it out loud—every word as if you are on stage. Just reading it entices us to read it quickly like reading a newspaper. Your eyes can miss errors you will hear if you speak the book. Invite a friend to read it to you. Invite friends to proof-read it. And, as novelist Kurt Vonnegut wrote, "Be merciless on yourself. If a sentence does not illuminate your subject in some new and useful way, scratch it out."[23] Does the structure flow effortlessly? Is every character or concept portrayed with the proper spirit, with a style that stirs the imagination of readers, engaging them like a painter and art patron together painting the same picture?

Be a Guardian of Your Characters

Great writers are fiercely loyal to the characters and concepts in their work. When Mahershala Ali gave his acceptance speech for the 2017 best supporting actor role in the movie **Moonlight**, he said: "It's not about you. It's about these characters. You're a service to these stories and these characters." It is not about falling in love with your characters and notions, although many writers do. Rather, it is about feeling a strong allegiance to ensuring they are properly and excellently represented to your reader. Duty can be a stimulating driver of your discipline.

William Zinsser, author of **On Writing Well**, wrote in his highly acclaimed book, "To defend what you've written is a sign that you are alive."[24] His plea is not to turn a deaf ear to critique but rather to invest so much of yourself in what you have created that you possess the glow of confidence and the strength of conviction. We all know our friends are not without flaws yet, we defend their honor. Treat your characters and concepts as your valued friends.

It's Not a Job, It's a Hobby

This is not about "one is hard; one is easy." Writing well can be very hard. This is about loving what you do. Treating your writing as your high-performance hobby means approaching it with joy and without stress. So, how do you do stressless writing?

1. Write every day, even if it is only for a few minutes. Again, it is okay to write badly. This is about the rhythm of the hobby,

not about its perfection. Even if you toss what you write, you are working on getting the engine of creativity running. Author George Singleton humorously wrote, "Keep a small can of WD-40 on your desk—away from any open flames—to remind yourself that if you don't write daily, you will get rusty."[25]

2. Start or join a writer's support group. Get a group of friends or colleagues to be your cheerleading team. If they are also writers, so much the better. When you are creating a book, the goal should be lots of affirmations—what they liked about your writing; when you are editing the book, the goal is feedback and suggestions. You will find a list of writer's support blog sites in the resource chapter at the end of this book.

3. Read, read, read. Find written works that inspire you. Blog sites like Success.com, TinyBuddha.com, Becomethelion.com, or AldenTan.com offer get-up-and-go encouragement. Reading helps introduce you to a variety of writing styles and character treatments. It also can help develop and refine your concepts. It introduces you to images that might influence or shape what you write. A concert pianist might play simple, easy children's songs to warm up before playing challenging compositions. Reading can be a great warm-up for creative writing.

4. Welcome visits in the middle of the night from your muse. If you go to bed thinking about your writing, you may be awakened with a great idea. Keep a writing pad by your bedside along with a tiny pen light. Do not wait until morning. Jot the idea down when it comes. Better still, get up and write as long

as you have the inspiration to do so. Poet Henry David Thoreau wrote, "Write while the heat is in you…the writer who postpones the recording of his thoughts uses an iron which has cooled to burn a hole with."[26]

5. Take care of the writer. You are not likely to write well if you are exhausted or distracted. Get sufficient rest and exercise. Even if it means walking around the block, get your heart pumping and your body energized. Write in a quiet place with little or no interruption or put on an audio headset and listen to music you enjoy but not music likely to cause you to "sing along." Noise canceling headphones work because they not only keep external sound out; they enhance the quality of what you hear.

Writing is a craft that requires continual honing. Like staying in physical shape, it works best when done continually, not occasionally. It will reward you with a product that will be a source of pride. But, writing excellence is a journey, not a destination. We only use a fraction of our mind's capacity; we use even less of our soul's reservoir of imagination. As Ernest Hemingway wrote: "We are all apprentices in a craft where no one ever becomes a master."[27]

Answer to the Square picture:

The first pattern your left brain recognizes is the sixteen squares in the figure. Then, your brain quickly reasons that there is one large square. With that discovery, you start counting 2 by 2 squares. Now, you are deep into the pattern and continue to reason. If you looked closely, there are nine of these in all.

Getting more advanced, your brain reasons that if 2 squares by 2 squares could produce nine, then 3 squares by 3 squares could yield even more. There are four. Adding up all of these you proudly announce the right answer is thirty.

But wait. Your right brain all along quietly wondered if there was more to the task than initially appeared. Could 'Count every square you see" mean more than the geometric pattern? The word "square" in the instructions should also be included in your calculation of squares seen. Your left brain now reacts as if it has been tricked. But, the creative side of your brain now realizes there are many squares in sight, not just the ones in this book. In our culture, the left brain is dominant; writing includes giving your right brain an equal chance to "see squares" so to speak.

Chapter 6

Book Construction Basics

"I'm not sure a bad person can write a good book.
If art doesn't make us better, then what on earth is it for."
—Alice Walker

"How do you construct a book?" is a bit like asking "How do you build a house?" There are a lot of "it depends." Yet, like building a house, there are basics every writer should know regardless of the book genre. All books start with an idea, ideally an inspired one. All books begin with a rough vision of a possibility the idea can be transformed into a book and what that book might be like. Rarely do writers start with a sentence and just haphazardly ramble their way to the closing line of a completed book. Here are a few tips to make your book writing flow more efficiently between idea and bookshelf.

Plan Your Book

Some fiction writers sketch out the storyline—the basic skeleton of the book—from start to finish. That means they know roughly how the plot turns out. Some authors—like short story, poetry, or some specialty book writers—write pieces and then assemble them in an appealing structure. Some authors decide on an organizational logic and tightly write to that structure. Let's use the book you are holding as a book planning organization example.

This book started with a target audience in mind—a new, aspiring writer who wanted to turn his or her writings into a published book. That choice dictated the book's complexity. There are books like this one that are more technical for the advanced or experienced writer; this book needed to be more introductory. Next, came the outline. The logic used was a linear sequence—much like a writer might encounter in the order writing challenges are most likely to occur.

Recognizing that the "how's" of writing vary by genre, we elected to put in the middle of the book a chapter on many of the common genres and then recruited genre experts to pen those particular chapters. It was also important that each chapter be about the same length (1,000-1,500 words) in order to create a sense of balance and frugality. We trusted that if readers wanted more about a particular topic they would seek out resources for greater depth.

Keep in mind that organization is driven by the tone and theme of the book. Charles Dickens opened his novel **The Tale**

of Two Cities with a chapter entitled, "Recalled to Life." It provided a tone-setter and context builder needed before starting the sequenced story of the events leading up to the French Revolution. Richard Adams' novel **Watership Down** opened with a tension-filled crisis faced by the characters before the book launched into their journey to escape and find a new life. Make certain you are thoughtful in how you lay out the book, remembering balance, tone, and symmetry help contribute to a pleasant experience for the reader.

Make Full Use of Tools for Organizing

Storyboards, mind maps, outlining lists, spreadsheets, transcription, and note cards are all tools that have been used by writers for many years to help organize their book. Today there are computer programs that make these familiar tools easier to use. *Storyboarding* is nothing more than a graphic organizer displayed in sequence for the purpose of pre-visualizing a book. It makes it easy to reorganize and build out each piece or chapter while keeping it clearly in context with the whole. It could be done on Microsoft PowerPoint. Poet Alice Friman suggests laying the book out on a long table.

Mind maps look like a small celled animal in a biology book! They are pictures that show the relationship between concepts in a hierarchy so that big ideas branch to smaller, supporting ideas. They are ideal for brainstorming. Some use words; some images and some both. *Outlining lists* and *spreadsheets* allow the creation of columns of concepts or ideas so they can be easily rearranged and interrelated. Microsoft Excel and Word are computer programs that can make listings and spreadsheets easy to maneuver and expand.

Transcription and *note cards* are essentially a means to capture ideas as they occur. Most smartphones have an app that allows you to speak an idea, a great advantage when driving. There is a computer program called Scrivener that helps you work with countless note cards using a drag-and-drop feature. It enables you to quickly see common threads that can be organized into a particular chapter. It can also be a tool to more easily enhance the logical flow of the book. Don't forget to consider placement of images, artwork or special graphics. Thinking ahead may impact how your organize the text.

Stop in a Place of Comfort

Writers sometimes forget their subconscious mind can be just as large an asset to any art form as their conscious mind. However, if the conscious mind is awake, alert, and active, the subconscious mind will remain in the background waiting for its turn to contribute. It is essentially kept sub (meaning underneath), only rising when the conscious mind has left the writing stage, so to speak.

Give your conscious mind a break so your subconscious can come out and play. Try not to think or worry about your writing when you are not physically writing. Having a daily word count limit is less important than stopping at a place where the writing in going well and you have a keen sense of where the writing is going next. During your non-writing time, your subconscious mind can take over, work on ideas, and be ready to contribute when your conscious mind resumes work.

Read Your Book Before Resuming Work

Ernest Hemingway wrote in a 1935 *Esquire* magazine article, "The best way is to read it all every day from the start, connecting as you go along, then go on from where you stopped the day before. When it gets so long that you can't do this every day, read back two or three chapters each day. Then, each week read it all from the start. That's how you make it all one piece."[28]

Hemingway's intent was not to recommend a process for rewriting or critiquing. It is rather a momentum-building approach to ensure continuity. It is also a way for the old content to be a foundation or platform on which to build the new content.

Be the Character; Live the Concept

Books are generally written about people, places, objects, and concepts. Think of these as the "pieces" around which the book is crafted. Success in all book genres comes from making the book pieces "come alive." It is the same craftsmanship used by great method actors.

When Sally Field and Daniel Day-Lewis starred in the hit movie **Lincoln**, they did not "play" Mary Todd Lincoln and Abraham Lincoln; they *were* these characters. According to movie director Stephen Spielberg, the actors stayed in character for the entire three months of shooting the movie. Day-Lewis insisted the cast and crew refer to him as "Mr. President." He called Sally Field, "Mrs. Lincoln" even when the two were not acting. It was immersion. Day-Lewis even refused to allow anyone with a British accent to speak with him out of fear it would "throw him off."

Your book deserves the same type of reverence and allegiance. When you are writing fiction, be the character about whom you are writing. When you are writing a non-fiction book about objects, places, or concepts, immerse your whole being into those pieces. Know them on a personal level. Be an expert on your pieces.

Study the nuance of every word to ensure it is the word that precisely captures the meaning and tone you want. Make heavy use of a thesaurus or the synonym checker on your computer's word processing program. For example, read the last sentence again. It uses the word "heavy." It could have instead used the word "weighty," "hefty," "full," "dense," or "thick." "Heavy" best conveyed the meaning. William Shakespeare could have written "Friends, Romans, and countryman, please listen up" as his opening line of Marc Antony's famous speech in *Julius Caesar*. We would never have remembered it. Instead, he used a more poetic, "lend me your ears," and it has been repeated for over four hundred years.

Artists are often lauded for their creativity but chastised for their lack of organization. They tend to continue to fiddle with the poetry or prose, avoiding closure. Novelist Truman Capote complained, "I never finished a book; someone came in and took it away from me." This more holistic, creative asset can make the more efficient, analytical side of crafting a book a necessary but highly tedious challenge. As one writer said, "I wish I had someone with an engineering mind to come clean up my mess." Yet, books do not write themselves. And, the artistry of authoring must at some point take a necessary backseat to the logic of book organization.

Chapter 7

The Surgical Side of Authoring

"The writer who breeds more words than he needs,
is making a chore for the reader who reads."
—Dr. Seuss

Elwyn Brooks "E. B." White is best known to the general public as the author of the children's books **Charlotte's Web** and **Stuart Little**. But, to writers, he is also known as the coauthor of the English language style book entitled **The Elements of Style**. "The best writing," wrote White, "is rewriting."

Famous authors with many helpers eager to edit their books still wrap up their first, second or third drafts and move from their role as creative writer to that of careful editor. Famed novelist Toni Morrison wrote: "Writers need rewriting and editing. It's as though you're in a laboratory and you're working on an experiment with chemicals or with rats, and it doesn't work. It doesn't mix. You don't throw up your hands and run out of the lab. What you do is you identify the procedure and what went wrong and then correct it. With writing, you can always write and erase and do it over."

What follows are a few cautions and suggestions about how to edit your own work. Many an acquisitions editor has turned down a promising manuscript simply because it is poorly edited. In the later chapter, "With a Little Help from Friends," there will be more detail about paid or professional editors. This chapter is for you as author wearing your best editor's visor.

Take a Break

Take a few days to clear your mind and recalibrate your pace from free-flowing invention to detailed scrutiny. During that time, congratulate yourself on completing your book draft. You have earned a break. The jolt of self-critique that is about to follow will be less painful if it happens along with a strong, affirmed self-esteem. Be proud and be prepared. Be like a championship figure skater, high-fiving yourself after a performance. Then ready yourself for the verdict rendered by you, the judge, or, as some writers refer to editors, "the butcher"!

Build Your Editor Momentum

Jumping in with a writing scalpel is never a good approach. Read through your book aloud. Using a listener is even better. Print a copy and read it again, lightly making notes in the margin about blatant errors, ideas, sections to move elsewhere, and places to review in more detail on your next read. Use spell-check. Some writers grew up with the practice of putting two spaces after a period that ended a sentence. Use "find and replace" to make certain there is only one space. For "find," put in two spaces; for "replace," put in one space. It makes your manuscript feel tighter and look more organized. The point is this: start with easy editorial tasks before taking on the necessary scalpel work in a line edit (or copyedit) where the color red is often involved.

Choose Solid Content over Ornate Style

Writers delight in the alliteration and poetry that flow from their keys or pen. And, most readers appreciate a clever turn of phrase. Done in excess, however, it can sound erudite and self-absorbed. Pretty sentences can sometimes detract from the flow of the book. Think of it this way. Your reader is on your book's path traveling from tension to resolution. The momentum is building as your reader anticipates the climax. Suddenly, the author detours to elegantly describe a unique flower along the path. While you think it would be entertaining to the reader, it is a distraction. Unless you are writing a poetry book, favor clear prose over extravagant poetry. Focus on nouns and verbs and let adjectives and adverbs remain in the background. To put it more strongly, question every adverb!

Do a Careful Word Review

Most word processing programs (like Microsoft Word) have a thesaurus feature. You simply paint the word in question, right-click on the computer, and cursor down to "synonyms." You might find another word that more accurately captures your intended meaning. Fundamentally, language is the transmission of meaning. Your goal is to select words that enable the imagery and meaning produced in the mind of the reader to match the imagery and meaning in the mind of the author.

Eliminate All Excesses

Excess slows the reader on his or her pathway to a conclusion, climax, or punchline. Author Peggy Noonan wrote, "Remember the waterfront shack with the sign, 'Fresh Fish Sold Here'? Of course, it's fresh, we're on the ocean. Of course, it's for sale, we're not giving it away. Of course, it's here, otherwise the sign would be someplace else. The final sign: 'Fish.'" Avoid what fiction writers call "throat clearing," i.e., spending too much time setting a scene or describing a character. Watch out for redundancies like "She shook her head from side to side *in disapproval*" "He stomped *his feet*" or "She blinked *her eyes*." Take out every single word that does not enhance the word picture in your reader's mind. For instance, examine these sentences: "She sat *down* at the table" or "He loaded *up* his backpack." Less is more.

Discovery Trumps Discourse

Novelist James Joyce advised leaving out some content to let the reader fill in the gaps. Discovery, that aha that comes from "getting it," is far more powerful than the understanding that follows an explanation or description. "Good writing is supposed to evoke sensation in the reader," wrote novelist E. L.

Doctorow. "Not the fact that it is raining, but the feeling of being rained on." Let emotion emerge from the content. This allows the reader to paint the picture through your direction. Compare these two sentences: "I hate you," Jill blurted out fiercely, her right hand clenched into a fist. Or, "I hate you," Jane said, her eyes narrowing. The first sentence requires no effort to get a clear picture. But, the second lets the reader use her or his imagination to surmise fury rather than be told fury.

Beta Readers to the Rescue

Beta readers are people you trust to give you solid and candid feedback. Solid feedback means readers that are uniquely qualified. For example, a military history novel might make reference to certain weapons. You will likely need someone with historical weapons expertise to weigh in on your technical accuracy. Candid feedback means someone willing to be honest in their assessment. Suggest they offer feedback from the perspective of a prospective reader. You might also want to include someone in your beta group who can proofread your manuscript to find typos, grammar infractions, and syntax errors. More on helpers will be explored in the chapter "With a Little Help from Friends."

Be an Editorial Sleuth

1. *Pace and rhythm are essential.* They are achieved by eliminating all unnecessary words plus shortening sentences. Cut, cut, cut. Readers read much faster than authors speak. Don't let your book drag. At the same time, give your readers an occasional mental break through short detours with a bit more

entertaining detail than needed. Fiction writer Terry Kay calls this a "flight of language."

2. *Watch out for "too many notes."* In the movie *Amadeus* when Wolfgang Mozart's opera *The Marriage of Figaro* was first performed, Emperor Joseph II, a musical novice, commented to Mozart at the end of the performance, "My dear young man, don't take it too hard. Your work is ingenious. It's quality work. And there are simply too many notes, that's all. Just cut a few and it will be perfect." It is likely you can delete twenty percent of your book and it will be perfect.

3. *Respect Your Reader.* Avoid trying to impress. Obtuse language is arrogant; you want to be just the opposite. Shun clichés and jargon. Err on the side of short words, concrete phrases over fancy ones. Stay on a constant hunt for typos. Guy Kawasaki and Shawn Welch relate a sad story in their book **APE**. When Penguin published a book called **The Pasta Bible** in 2010, the recipe for tagliatelle called for "salt and freshly ground black people." Obviously, spell-check missed it. Penguin had to destroy seven thousand copies because of one word. Typos not only can have grave consequences, they can signal carelessness to your reader.

4. *Punctuation is the arbitrator of meaning.* A missing comma or one in the wrong place can completely alter the reader's interpretation of your meaning. Proper hyphenation can mean the difference between working twenty-four hour shifts, twenty four-hour shifts, or twenty-four-hour shifts. Read that again! Sprinkling in a comma where none belongs can turn a Panda's

diet ("eats shoots and leaves") into a dastardly act ("eats, shoots and leaves").[29] Avoid using semicolons where commas should be. Semicolons typically connect two independent clauses when conjunctions are not used.

5. *Tone needs to match the topic.* Use active, not passive voice whenever possible. STOP yelling at your reader by putting words in all caps or using unexpected punctuation. If most sentences end with an explanation point, the reader quickly tires and the punctuation is ultimately ineffective. F. Scott Fitzgerald wrote, "An explanation point is like laughing at your own joke." Be careful of point-of-view changes that leave readers confused about the character speaking or the real subject.

6. *Avoid Use of Problem Words.* If you are unsure of whether it is then or than, look it up. **Grammar Girl's Quick and Dirty Tips for Better Writing** zeros in on these problem words: *good* or *well, anxious* or *eager, alot* or *a lot, effect* or *affect, further* or *farther, it's* or *its, that* or *who, their, there* or *they're, less* or *fewer, i.e.* or *e.g., who* or *whom, your* or *you're,* and *can* or *may.* Another type of problem word is the type few readers understand. John Grisham says, "There are three types of words: 1) words we know, 2) words we should know, and 3) words nobody knows. Forget those in the third category and use restraint with those in the second. A common mistake by fledgling authors is using jaw-breaking vocabulary. It's frustrating and phony."[30]

"The beautiful part of writing," said author Robert Cormier, "is that you don't have to get it right the first time, unlike, say, a brain surgeon." So, write without worry, read without silence, and edit without mercy.

Books come in many types—called genres. Genre comes from a French word meaning "kind." Genres are categories of books that share a similar form, style, or subject and there are many book genres. The next eight chapters to follow provide an overview of that genre coupled with tips, techniques, and advice from authors who have been successful writing in their chosen genres. Not covered are genres like children's books, biographies, mysteries, science fiction, and many others. Future editions or versions of this book will explore more genres. All of the authors featured in this book live in the Lake Country area near the Georgia Writers Museum.

Chapter 8
How to Write Fiction
Interview with Terry Kay

"It is only a novel... or, in short, only some work in which the greatest powers of the mind are displayed, in which the most thorough knowledge of human nature, the happiest delineation of its varieties, the liveliest effusions of wit and humor, are conveyed to the world in the best-chosen language."

–Jane Austen

The words are from famed novelist Jane Austen. And, one of the few people on this planet who understands the hard work and disciplined wisdom needed to deliver a truly great novel is Terry Kay. His many novels are as provocative as they are renowned. Chip spent the morning with this best-selling Georgia Hall of Fame novelist, appropriately in a small reading room in a public library near his home. Here are a few passages from the interview.

What made you choose fiction as your writing genre?

"My background from college is theater, not literature, and it's always been the influence that drives my understanding of fiction. But what created my choice of fiction as my genre was a prank orchestrated by my good friends, novelist Pat Conroy and *Atlanta Magazine* founding editor Jim Townsend. Pat had tried for a long time to get me to write fiction. I saw it as a lifelong sentence in an Alcatraz of words instead of an opportunity. Pat told Jim he knew a way to trick me into writing fiction.

"He called his editor, Anne Barrett, at Houghton Mifflin. Anne had been the American editor for **Lord of the Rings** author, J.R.R. Tolkien, and was working with Pat at the time on his book **The Great Santini.** Pat told Anne he had just finished reading 150 pages of a manuscript his friend Terry Kay was writing. He loved it and thought they should see it. I obviously had not written anything and did not know about his phone call until a few days later when I received a letter from Anne begging to see my 150-page manuscript Conroy was raving about.

"I went to Pat's house and yelled at him. He just let me rave and then said, 'Kay, you can do one of two things: you can reply to her and tell her I was drunk and you don't have anything at all or, you can write 150 pages.' Well, he knew what I would do.

"I grew up in a large family in Royston, GA, with parents who taught us: 'If someone expresses faith in you, you have an obligation to try.' In one month, I wrote 150 pages on an old manual typewriter. I sent her the manuscript with an honest letter saying I did not think it was any good. I knew they would turn it down and I could get Conroy off my back. To my shock, she offered me a contract and a small advance to write a novel based on one little vignette in the 150 pages. **The Year the Lights Came On** was published in 1976.

Where do your best initial ideas come from?

"Curiosity. The ideas come from chance, momentary encounters with something you didn't expect. It can come from anyone and anything. There is no set pattern. It is something that happens, the epiphany of a moment.

Before you write, do you prepare an outline? Do you organize around a plot?

"I write to discover a story, rather than to tell one that's been set in stone, therefore I don't start with an outline, though I might structure one halfway through a story, but it's one that goes backward, rather than forward, simply because I want to keep the foundation straight in my thinking. Discovery, for me, is the source of energy. If the characters are interesting, I can find the story.

Once you have characters in mind and the start of a theme, does the book sort of write itself? Do you pretty much know where it is going?

"I have no idea where it's heading initially and I don't want to know. I would be bored to death since I would discover nothing.

Writing fiction involves a basic question: "What if. . .?" Writing is a simple thing; we make it complicated. And, frankly I believe the only place you are going to learn to write is in front of a machine. I can share with you certain techniques that have helped me but I cannot teach someone to write. It's not about just putting words on a page; that's a typist. Being a good writer is something you earn through hard work. Frankly, novel writing begins with the third draft; by that I mean the third complete rewrite.

What makes for good novel writing in your view?

"The DNA of writing consists of three things. First, know what a verb is. Verbs are the power of the senses. When writing, ask yourself, 'Can it be seen or heard? How does the verb relate this?' Second, know how to use rhythm. Rhythm engages rather than bores the reader. Seventy percent of great writing is rhythm, which is nothing more than the length of sentences. And, third, pay attention to word selection. It's not about overwhelming the reader with your brilliance, your knowledge, or your gift of language. It's about paying conscious attention to the work – and it is work.

What would be an example of keeping your reader engaged?

"Every fifteen or twenty pages I find a place for a 'flight of language.' Sometimes it's for my own pleasure. But, mainly it is to say to the reader: 'This is not from a romance or mystery writer; this is from someone who is writing a story, hopefully with some lyricism to it, that will ask you to go on a journey of discovery with him.'

What are ways you make your characters come alive?

"Paying attention to the power and influence of dialogue. I believe I can describe a person through the use of dialogue better than through narrative. You would not have a rural Southerner using the same language as an Irishman. Listen for the language and be faithful to the sound of it. The reader is likely to hear it also and in his/her imagination will subconsciously become part of the story.

What is your advice to an aspiring novelist?

"Learn to listen with curiosity. Learn the art of imitation. I learned how to write as a young sports writer for the *Atlanta Journal*. Furman Bisher was a sports columnist and perhaps the finest writer I have ever met face to face. Every night, I would copy the column he had written that day, and in so doing I began to understand something of his immense talent. Get a book you like—a good one, not trash – and copy it. When you finish it, you will be a far better writer than you've ever been.

"Some other suggestions: Be attentive to elements that have nothing to do with your emotional attachment to the story. You need to know when you are writing an intrusion. Does the story work best in first or third person?

What is the one final thought you would give an aspiring novelist?

"Writing a novel takes passion, but it's not the dreamy, romantic experience you hear about — that outburst of chest-thumping so many writers declare in social media. The passion I'm suggesting is from that mysterious source that drives your tenacity, your discipline and your resilience, the type that pushes you to strive for a memorable finished product, not just a hot-topic story that reviewers might label as good. Your passion should represent the passion of your characters so thoroughly that they would rise up and applaud you because you truly understood their story and told it with the integrity that gave them a valued voice.

Chapter 9

How to Write Non-Fiction

By Lisa Earle McLeod

"If uncovering the truth is the greatest challenge of nonfiction writing, it is also the greatest reward."

—Candice Millard

I hated to write when I was in school. In fact, I applied to the University of Georgia because, at the time, it was one of the few colleges that didn't require an essay. Years of teachers critiquing my poor spelling, my incorrect grammar, my horrible handwriting and my endless typos had convinced me I couldn't write. I'm a graduate of the UGA School of Journalism, who majored in broadcast and management so she could avoid writing whenever possible.

Flash forward a decade and a half from college. I'm all grown up, I'm married with kids, and I'm a sales consultant. One Christmas I got one of those horrible, over-the-top holiday letters. You know the kind: Bill got promoted and now runs the Universe, Sandy is at Harvard getting straight A's, little Mikey is an opera protégé, and here are our photos from Hawaii. It was totally nauseating.

I thought, someone should write a holiday letter about real life. Then I thought, maybe that someone is me. So, I did. I wrote letters about our kids getting head lice and giving it to the entire swim team. I wrote about the Orkin® man telling us he wouldn't come back to treat our ants again if we kept leaving half-eaten lollipops on the table. And I wrote about how my daughter hated soccer and refused to come off the bench, because "you have to run too much."

I sent it out along with a candid photo of our kids with snotty noses. Within days, people were calling me laughing out loud. Keep in mind, this was in the early 2000's, before the wave of mommy bloggers ewho xposed the dirty secrets of motherhood, and before people put their holiday greetings on Facebook. This was hard copy, and it was funny. The next year I did another one, and soon people were asking me to send multiple copies so they could share them.

Armed with the wild success of three holiday letters, I thought I would try my hand at writing a non-fiction book.

I was naïve but was at least smart enough to recognize that the leap from holiday letters to a full-fledged book is quite a jump.

That's where my friend JoAnn Neely came in. She had a master's degree, she'd done a thesis; she knew how to write. We originally thought JoAnn would write the book; I was the idea person.

Yet as our journey progressed, we discovered that once I shook off my self-imposed filters, I could make the words on a page sing.

I got two pieces of advice that transformed my relationship with writing.

The first was from a friend who said, "Just write like you talk." This was novel to me. I didn't know you were allowed to do that. I thought you had to be all writerly and stuff. Yet when I thought back to the books I enjoyed most, they weren't scholarly books; they were like talking to a good friend.

The next piece of transformational advice came from Chip Bell, the author of this book and a longtime friend and mentor, who said, "Sit at your keyboard, put some music on and listen to the voice." That single suggestion was a game changer.

Chip listens to Italian opera and Southern gospel. For me, it was Carole King and Abba who unlocked the part of my brain that had something meaningful to say. The year I started working on *Forget Perfect*, my husband bought me a new music system for my office. I spent the next six weeks working late into the night banging away to "I Feel the Earth Move" and "Dancing Queen." The ideas and the emotions flew out of me. I loved every minute of it.

I had two little kids and a day job. But you wouldn't know it when I hit the keyboard. Staying up until 2 or 3 am writing wasn't drudgery, it was magic. I can honestly say it was one of the most exciting times of my life. For the first time ever, there was no time limit, there was no one coming afterward to correct me, and there was no worry about what other people would think. Once I let go of my expectation that I had to write like a writer, I could pour my heart into it.

Non-fiction does not mean non-emotional. I was originally inspired to write a book because I saw and experienced a problem that broke my heart. Every woman I knew, including me, was making herself crazy trying to be all things to all people, yet constantly feeling like she never measured up. The women who stayed home, the women who worked, and the women like me, who did some of both—we were all making ourselves nuts trying to be perfect at everything yet not enjoying a minute of it.

That was the issue calling to me.

What is the challenge calling to you? Many people write books because they want to boost their business. A book can and should help you improve your brand and business. But if that's your primary motivation, I can promise you right now, your book will probably be boring. As someone who now writes about books, I have books come across my desk every day that were obviously written by someone who wanted to prove their 'thought leadership.'" They are universally formulaic and uninspiring. That's because they're about the author. Good books are about the *reader*. A good non-fiction book uses the author's experiences and perspective to help the reader, not impress the reader.

As you think about your book, think about what's out there that's bothering you. What issue do you see that's not getting enough attention? What solutions do you wish more people knew about? What would be helpful for people to know? What inspires you?

For me writing a book is a labor of love. I often say, I only write a book when I'm so annoyed about a problem that it's easier to write the damn book than to not to write the book. I'm not as prolific as many writers, but every book I've written has meant something to me. It's probably not a coincidence that they've also all done fairly well.

I see nonfiction book writing as divided into three parts:

The writing itself, which can and should be emotional, at least if you want it to be interesting. The writing comes from your sincere desire to improve something.

Editing, which needs to be ruthless and practical. I favor the famous editor saying, sometimes you have to kill your darlings. I used to write at night and edit in the clear light of day.

Last, selling, which is about finding a market and winning it. This takes discipline, lots of work and is rarely accomplished overnight. To get non-fiction published, you must demonstrate a need and a market. To sell your non-fiction book, you must actively and continually engage with potential readers.

Writing and getting published are not easy. If they were everyone would have a book. But if you think about it, nothing meaningful in life is easy. If you have something to say, you deserve to be heard. Writing a book is a chance to make a difference. You never know how your book will impact the lives of your readers. It may wind up being more important to someone than you ever dreamed.

So, write like a lover, edit like a teacher, and sell your work as if someone's life depends on it.

Chapter 10

Writing for
The News Media

By Mark Engel

"We cannot make good news out of bad practice."

—Edward R Murrow

Writing News stories for TV, Radio, Print or the Internet is non-fiction storytelling at its fastest, freshest and least forgiving. You have little time to research it, write it and edit it before it is immediately sent out to an audience that is probably larger and more critical than will ever see your first published book.

It is a trip into the world of Fake News, where there are "facts" and "alternative facts" that are often confused by a veneer of bias and opinion.

69

When done correctly, writing real News stories will be extremely exciting, instantly rewarding and, oh yeah, fun.

The deadlines are short but that doesn't mean you ignore the key elements of any well-written book. You still need the Facts, the Opinion, and the Characters.

The Facts

In Breaking News situations, Facts come fast and furious from different sources:

- House fire kills three people.
- The mayor suffered chest pains.

As a journalist, it is your job to sort through the information and tell your story with as much accuracy as you can. Your credibility depends on it. Pretend the reader is looking over your shoulder, asking "Where-did-you-get-that-Fact?"

Remember, you can never be absolutely sure that a Fact is really a Fact unless you know, first hand, it is true.

The best thing to do with Facts that you cannot independently confirm is to attribute them to the source:

- Thomasville fire dispatcher Mary Jones said three people were killed.
- City Manager Tom Smith said the mayor suffered chest pains.

Confirming sources is not just important in Breaking News situations.

I once reviewed a script prior to it being broadcast on CNN. It was a feature story about a steam engine train that operates a regularly scheduled route in Liberia. The owner told our reporter it was the only regularly scheduled steam engine train in the world.

I required him to attribute the claim to the owner of the train service. Sure enough, when the story aired around the world we got a call from a Canadian who said he operates a regularly scheduled steam engine train route also.

Even in soft, feature-type stories, the Facts can be elusive.

The Opinion

Many stories you will write will be important because of the new information they provide:

- new gun control legislation
- automobile recall

Never allow yourself to think a story or an issue is straightforward because there are likely people who have differing Opinions about it. Your job is to seek out viewpoints from different sides of the story and determine how many, if any, are to be included in your story.

- A new gun control bill will find many supporters who think too many people are being murdered. A vocal opposition will feel it violates the U.S. Constitution.
- An automotive recall causes safety concerns but the car company says injuries are not their fault.

You will not be able to include all the Facts and all the Opinions in your story. You must balance everything you have.

Always keep in mind the adage that "everyone is entitled to their own Opinion but not their own Facts."

The Characters

Your News story may not impact everyone in your audience, but how important can a story be if it does not affect anyone?

I once read a story about traffic congestion in a big city. There were many Facts about commuter wait times, road construction costs, and comparisons with other cities. The mayor, the police chief, and someone from the highway department had comments.

But, the reporter did not talk to any motorists, small business owners whose business is hurt by traffic or the guy in the toll booth who hears the gripes of angry drivers every day. The story communicated Facts but it lacked the emotion necessary to connect with the audience.

You must find and talk to real, ordinary people who are impacted by the issue you are reporting.

Writing the News Story

At this point, you don't have much time left before your deadline!

If you are reporting for television, you must write a story that takes maximum advantage of the video that will be used. A radio reporter considers the audio. Print journalists from Newspapers to Internet blogs must think about pictures and graphics that will be alongside the article.

But all the media magic in the world will not help a poorly told story.

Begin your story by introducing a person or persons affected by your story. You don't need to spend a lot of time. Just enough to get the audience to be interested in them and their connection to the topic.

> NOTE: The following story was created as a short example. None of the content is factual.

Every Tuesday, Thursday, and Saturday, 68-year old Brenda Willington musters up enough energy to climb into her car and drive three hours to Johnsonville hospital for chemo-therapy treatment. She has been doing this for two years, since being diagnosed with lung cancer.

Then, report the facts of the bigger story. Tell what is new information. Give details.

Willington and the 20 million other Americans like her who are trying to stay alive with chemotherapy may be getting some relief.

The American Lung Association reports that a pill that can replace chemotherapy treatments has shown an effective rate of 85 percent in tests.

According to research conducted at the Greg Cancer Insti-tute, the pill, when taken daily, attacks the cancer cells with ten times as much impact as chemotherapy, without the side effects.

If the issue raises a controversy or spawns Opinions on multiple sides, you should report those views. While you don't have to count words, you should do your best to balance conflicting comments.

> But, Dr. Mark Thomas, the head of research at Jefferson Cancer Institute, is skeptical of the report. "I've been looking for cancer cures for forty-two years now and to think that the answer can come, all of a sudden, in a pill is ludicrous," he said. Thomas also points out that the study's findings are based on tests conducted on fewer than one hundred patients.

> US Secretary of Health and Cancer Studies Gerri Horn says she has reviewed the findings and believes them to be credible. She is authorizing a $52 million grant to speed up the process of final research and government approval.

At the end of the story, it is important to return to the person you introduced at the beginning. Wrap up their story into a package that when delivered to your audience will be informative, interesting, accurate and fair.

> Until that happens, Brenda Willington will continue to spend three full days a week keeping herself alive with chemotherapy and hoping for a day when help can be delivered to her door in a pill bottle.

You will probably get feedback only if someone thinks you made a mistake.

But the good News about writing stories for the News media is that the next day you get to start all over and do it again.

Chapter 11
Writers of
Inspirational Books
by John P. Dennis

"If you can't, you must. If you must, you can."
—Anthony Robbins

Inspirational books set out to inspire, motivate and uplift. They are commonly linked to religious or spiritual materials and therefore must contend with major authorities that may have addressed the author's subject already. From Jesus to the Dalai Lama, the inspirational author joins a highly respected cadre of authors that regard the mind, emotions, spirit and nature of mankind. This creates a central need for trust between reader and author built on credibility, insight and value that cannot be understated.

There is also a bit of a blurry line between Inspirational and Motivational books. A summarization of Google searches on the difference in the definitions averages out to... inspiration is something you feel on the inside while motivation is from the outside that compels action. Whether you write in a motivational or inspirational pattern, the core elements remain the same.

Establish Credibility

Credible research, stats, and sources help an author support the main theme of the book. Invoking powerful authorities such as the Bible or major influential figures such as Anthony Robbins create a foundation of borrowed credibility to build upon. Ph.D.'s and lofty associations are not the only way to attain credibility in this genre. Life experience, suffering and overcoming significant obstacles also prove to be reliable credentials for inspired writers. A mother of seven can be just as influential and respected as a college professor. Readers need to believe that you are an authority on your content, so don't fail to establish your credibility.

Give Them What They're Looking For

Anne Hart said it this way, "What the religious or inspirational markets are looking for is sharing what you've learned from your mistakes or experiences, how you arrived at your choices, and how you've grown and were transformed, gaining wisdom that everyone can share. By sharing your experiences and life story, readers will learn how you made decisions and why, what wisdom you gained from your growth or transformation, and what made it possible for you to grow and change and become a stronger and better person. The stories you'd write about would be those universal messages we all go through, such as rites of passage, dealing with the stages of life in new ways, finding alternatives, and how you handled the challenges."[31]

Readers are not just looking for solutions. They also need affirmation that they can achieve the same results, new ways to view situations that may never change and details about the ups and downs of the journey. When you show readers the process, the rewards, and the possibilities for personal growth, they are escorted to a belief that they can do it and will succeed.

Make Believers Out of Them

Share a healthy number of related challenges and shortcomings that you deal with so that you are not superhuman. By using anecdotes and examples, the grand ideas presented become real and attainable. You can easily dehumanize a book and make it an academic exercise or a book on suffering written by Superman. Your vulnerability is often what readers connect to and remember.

Include Exercises and Summaries

Rick Warren sold over 30 million copies by taking readers on a 40-day spiritual journaling experience in **The Purpose Driven Life**. The power of making the book partially written by the reader and acted upon weaves a deep connection for author and reader to enjoy. Principles, experiences, and lessons learned can be highlighted or boxed in to stand out for readers who flip through table of contents and chapters looking for great ideas that grab their attention. In similar fashion, end-of-chapter summaries provide quick reference to your core principles and takeaways that make the material memorable and digestible. Exercises also make your readers a part of the storyline and give them reference points to judge themselves against your major principles.

Why Inspirational Books Sell

There are 5 main reasons inspirational books sell.
1. Celebrity/Fame of the Author
2. Solves a Problem
3. Entertaining
4. Provides New Insight
5. Word of Mouth

Comedian/Actor and Talk Show Host Steve Harvey tapped into the power of Celebrity when he released **Straight Talk, No Chaser.** By promoting your book's strongest selling points, all of your marketing materials including the cover will bind together a cohesive effort to publicize your most attractive features. It must be evident what issue you are addressing, solving or just examining on initial glance to capture the attention of your target audience or the casual sampler. FYI, Word of Mouth is the most powerful method to finding your audience, so don't fail to ask for shares on FB, pastes for links on social media profiles and book reviews at every opportunity.

By establishing credibility with your audience, sharing the details and process of your journey, then leveraging your most attractive dynamic, you pave the road that creates a receptive audience glued to your insight, solutions and perspective they might never have entertained without these persuasive underpinnings. This sets the stage for the inspirational writer and ensures the essential ingredients of a compelling book that readers will enjoy.

"The dreamers are the saviors of the world. As the visible world is sustained by the invisible, so men, through all their trials and sins and sordid vocations, are nourished by the beautiful visions of their solitary dreamers."

—James Allen, *As a Man Thinketh*

Chapter 12

A Short Guide to Short Story Writing

by George Heiring

*"A short story is the ultimate close-up magic trick –
a couple of thousand words to take you around the universe
or break your heart."*
—Neil Gaiman

Every ascending journey to authorship needs a starting point. For many writers—those who achieved literary fame as well as those getting under way—short stories have proven to be an effective launching pad to publication. In the span of the first page or two, short stories reveal a writer's ability to attract a reader's attention and focus it on a single theme, a brief plot and a small cast of characters. They give seasoned wordsmiths a way to sharpen their skill and attract a following. Their greater appeal for many writers is that they will actually *finish* a short story, not always the case when they undertake a novel or an epic poem.

How Short Is "Short"?

Edgar Allan Poe defined a short story as a piece of fiction that can be read in one sitting. Kurt Vonnegut impishly advised short story writers to "start as close to the end as possible." While length can fuel a luncheon debate, modern short stories generally fall within a range of 1,000 to 20,000 words. If you are hoping to be published, keep in mind magazines and anthologies give priority to those with fewer than 5,000 words, especially if the author is not widely known.

Don't Talk It—Write It!

Are you brimming with ideas and experiences that beg to be shared? If so, do your best to share them via the written word. Rehashing your favorite tales for friends and family may deprive you of your incentive to write them. Think of your story as a delicious, fresh banana. Don't peel it and let it turn brown before its ready to be consumed.

Riding Inspiration, Driving Motivation

There are two horses in your creative stable, the fleet-footed filly *Inspiration* and the powerful workhorse *Motivation.* You begin your ride on Inspiration at full gallop, words and images coming quickly to your imaginative mind. You may find yourself chuckling at a witty phrase or bit of dialogue just escaped from your keyboard. You may punch the air as the action in your plot gets hot. A tear may leak from your eye when your story takes a tragic turn. At the quarter turn, when Inspiration is in full stride, the joy and spontaneity of storytelling is an almost narcotic high. *My gosh*, you hear yourself confessing, *this is really good.*

Before reaching the clubhouse turn, Inspiration has begun to fade, worn down by the ongoing grind of the what stays, what goes editing process. You may hear yourself asking *is anyone going to want to read this?* As your pace begins to slow, you will need a dose of fresh perspective and an injection of positive outlook. Time to harness up the plow horse Motivation to help you reach the finish line.

Here are a couple of ideas to spur you along:

- Once you have finished your day's allotment of writing, add one more sentence to the page to remind you where you intend for your story to go. The next day, that sentence will show up on the blank page to serve as a guiding light.

- Each day, before you begin to write, read what you have already produced. Read it out loud. Is the piece conveying your intended meaning? Are the cadence, construction and flow communicating your ideas clearly and memorably? If not, start editing. Then read it again and edit some more.

- When you have completed your first draft, read it to someone who will give you candid feedback—a friend, spouse, or members of your writing group. Observe their reactions to see if they match your intent. Do the readers look puzzled, pleased, shocked, amused or a bit bleary-eyed? When you finish reading, ask what in the story was most memorable. What was confusing?

Sing Your Song Your Way

Ernest Hemingway offered his stories in a straightforward manner famously devoid of adjectives. His contemporary William Faulkner expressed himself more emotionally and subtly in long, complex sentences and page-long paragraphs. Whose literary style will work best for you? Yours! Your voice is unique and relevant—no need to lip-sync someone else. Sing your song your way.

Your Tool Box: Short Story Essentials

- *Catch the Reader's Eye:* Your first—and best—opportunity to attract reader interest comes instantly and fleetingly as they glance at the title of your story or the illustration (if any) that accompanies it. In the lingo of modern rap, "If you don't catch their eye, readers pass by." Keep honing, reinventing your title until it is irresistible.

- *Hook the Reader's Attention for At Least Twenty Seconds:* Your first paragraph is critical. You are asking readers to give you their time and attention, while, in fact, they have a thousand other tempting places to invest them. Short stories imply something will happen quickly. To keep that promise, you have approximately twenty seconds to sell interest in your tale and prevent your audience from tuning out.

- *Use Lively, Unexpected Words:* "His fist *hit* the table." Really? Why not pounded, punched, smacked, slapped, thumped, cuffed or rapped? All convey a different intensity and motif that give that dull sentence sharper focus. Assuming your word processor is equipped with a thesaurus app, make it your lifelong pal. Consult it to find alternatives for words with too little tread left on them.

- *Your Prose Is Your Concerto:* Give your story variety of pace and intensity as if it were a musical composition— blasts of fortissimo, passages of pianissimo. Inject some moments of conflict, problems to be solved, challenges to overcome, characters readers can cheer or boo.

- *Create an Ending That Will Linger in Memory.* Leave your reader hungry for more. Close with a strong paragraph or line. Offer a surprise. Leave with a laugh. Think of ways to bridge back to your title or opening paragraph. Your readers have chosen to spend time with you. Make sure they look forward to a return visit.

Many writers yearn for publication. Few achieve it. Short stories are an excellent way to get you on track toward becoming an author. Once you start writing, you'll find the fleet-footed filly Inspiration is pawing the turf, anxious to take you for an exciting ride. So, giddy up!

Chapter 13

The Bottom Line on Writing a Business Book

by Chip R. Bell

"Writing is an act of faith, not a trick of grammar."
—E. B. White

Business books are written primarily to instruct and prompt action. Business books sell primarily because they inspire, entertain, and influence. Business books, like business in general, typically have a financial return objective attached. While many business writers enjoy the sheer experience of writing, if there is not a likelihood of an economic return, they are less likely to invest the energy needed to bring their business book to market.

Business books are more than just written material for people in the world of work. They can be a catalyst that helps change the way commerce is done. As such, business books indirectly impact everyone, not simply individual readers seeking entertainment. Tom Peters' and Bob Waterman's best-selling book **In Search of Excellence**, for example, dramatically transformed the way organizations operated for many years because of the book's influence on the leaders who read it.

Make It Unique

There are over 20,000 business books published every year—that's over fifty new titles a day. And, that quantity is growing! The competition for business book sales is fierce. Why? Most business subjects have been covered a lot. For example, if you were writing a book on leadership, you would learn that Amazon carries over 200,000 books with "leadership" in the title. If you want a book that has a chance of being accepted by a book agent or publisher (or being purchased if you self-publish), your approach to your subject must be something your buyer will view as different.

There are many forms of unique. Let's say you enjoy playing pick-up basketball in your neighborhood. You realize that influencing folks to join your team for an afternoon game is a good metaphor for leadership. You think of calling the book **Leading Three Pointers.** Your key principles might be—No Trouble in the Huddle, Retrench the Bench, Rebound Teamwork, or Locker Room Magic, etc. That's unique. The point is to offer readers a brand-new topic or an old topic presented in a brand-new way. We will focus on selling your unique book in a later chapter!!

Make It Relevant

Business book readers are generally seeking tools to solve a problem, perspectives to enrich their thinking, or practices to enhance their skills. While there are business book readers with the same pleasure-seeking goal as the reader of a romance novel on vacation, most have a pragmatic goal in mind. Relevance is therefore key to holding these readers' attention. It means no wandering far afield from your storyline. It involves selecting examples that offer concrete illustration, not just ones that entertain. It means writing in a manner that delivers fast-paced reading. Staying grounded and on point are essential.

The other side of relevance is timeliness. Like music, clothes, and cars, business books that sell reflect the current interests of the target audience. It requires taking time to do your homework on issues discussed, challenges lamented, and successes celebrated to get a bead on what's hot. Read business periodicals or websites—*Wall Street Journal*, *Forbes*, *Fast Company*, *Bloomberg Businessweek*, *Entrepreneur*, *Financial Times*, *Inc. Magazine* and watch business TV channels like CNBC, Bloomberg TV, and Fox Business. Keep asking yourself: How will my book help readers better deal with their work issues and concerns?

Make It Solid

The business world thrives with order, structure, organization, standards, and metrics. Excellence comes when a collection of talented people works collaboratively towards a common, captivating mission much like a well-oiled machine. Your book needs to possess these same features. It takes a linear structure in which each key concept builds on the one before. It requires a book organization that makes complete sense to the reader.

Solid means a book that fulfils its implied promise. Remember, most readers buy business books with a result in mind. Provide a clear framework chock full of how-to ways to immediately implement your suggestions. Keep this goal in mind: What do I want my reader to do (or do better) when she or he completes my book? If you write a pure feel-good book, it might make you feel good, but it will not likely make your bank account feel any better! Business book readers are impatient and eager to get to the punch line—a finale that must be worth their trip through all the words to get there.

Axioms for Business Writing You Won't Learn from the *Wall Street Journal*

Examining the style of business books that sell reveals their style is different from the *Harvard Business Review* or the *Wall Street Journal*. It is the difference between watching CNBC and watching the Discovery Channel. Business reporter-talk, the kind you find in business magazines and newspapers, is typically fact-based, fast-paced, rather sterile, and grounded in objective data. Business people turn to them for a briefing, not for an education or for inspiration. Here are twelve principles that might help balance a style that is relevant and solid with one that is compelling and insightful.

1. Metaphors create word pictures in the reader's mind that make the message memorable. Use them generously, but not without purpose.

2. The sound of the words is important. Write as if your book will be read from a stage and the audience will not have a copy.

3. Strong stories will be remembered long after solid facts have been forgotten. You should tell stories like someone's grandfather, not like an expert.

4. The poetry of the language should never, ever take a backseat to the logic of the content. Remember "lend me your ears?" Not really logical, but long remembered.

5. Business books should be experienced as novels, not as big white papers or business reports for board members. Business is an adventure filled with exciting illustrations and a sense of theater; business books should be likewise.

6. The biggest difference between a business book and a business manual is charm.

7. Clarity is crucial; color is even more important. So is clever writing.

8. Simplicity always trumps complexity in the memory of the reader. Complex is reserved for professors who are eager to profess their wisdom in a classroom.

9. Never take away from the reader the elements of magic, mystery, and charm.

10. Giving appropriate credit cannot ever be slighted. Cites, permissions, and references must be thorough and exact.

To the reader, it is called "integrity." To the writer, it is called "staying out of court!"

11. If the message is heavy, the style should be light; if the content is complex, its explanation should be simple.

12. Books should be experienced as messages to readers. As a writer, you are a messenger, not the message.

Bottom line, a great business book is crafted around "one big idea." If someone asks you what your new book is about and you cannot answer in one sentence, you need to more tightly focus your thinking and writing. An effective business book is a thin slice of a narrow topic crafted to compel action. As such it is more essence than encyclopedia, more like the spark plug of action than the engine of change.

Chapter 14

Poetry Advice 101

by Alice Friman

"What dream needs finishing? what story told?"

—Alice Friman

You want to know how to write a book of poems? Well, the first thing you need to do is write *a lot* of poems. That way not only will you have a great many to choose from to include in your book, but after you make your selection, you'll end up with a group of your *best* poems, poems you've brooded over and polished up for years. A book of poetry is like a chain that's only as good as its weakest link, which is to say, a poetry collection is only as good as its weakest poem, so no fillers, no not-so-hot ones thrown in there because you want to fill up a section or you want to include a certain poem because the situation it tells about has sentimental value for you, like your first kiss or your mama's beatific smile. No, each poem must shine on its own terms.

Selecting poems for your book is not the time for sentimentality. Some of your poems might be old ones and you will have to decide if they fit with the newer work. You need to take a good hard look at what you've got. Spread them all out on the floor perhaps, or a very long table, to get an overview of what you have. It might surprise you to see what you have been saying or trying to say unconsciously for these past, let's say, four or five years. You might be taken aback. Because poetry doesn't lie and comes from the deepest part of you, you might be surprised, pleasantly or otherwise, at the emotional expressions of who you are and who and what and where you've been.

Once you've done that—taken a good clear look at what you have—you need to cull out the weakest pieces and the poems that seem like doubles, which is to say, the ones that duplicate others. Sometimes, that's difficult. Often, beginning writers tend to think their poems are like their children and cannot bear to let any of them go. Perhaps they think everything they write is good and worthy. Think again. You are creating a work of art, and putting a collection together is the one time you need to be tough on yourself.

Now comes the most difficult part: how to organize the manuscript. This is especially problematic for a collection of poetry, because, unlike a novel or piece of long fiction, each piece was written separately at a different time and place, and each one is unique or should be. After all, everyone, especially a poet, is a multifaceted person; thus, a collection of poems will reflect the various sides of the author, his proclivities, her unique take on the world. The opening poems need to be especially powerful to engage the reader. The powers that be used to say it's important to front- load the manuscript—putting the strongest poems first. Personally, I think ALL the poems need to be strong, from first to last. A book of poems should be organized so that the whole book IS a poem. The way to do that is to create an arc, an umbrella under which all the work fits. If you choose to divide the book into sections, then each section should be an arc. Each section organized the way you'd organize a reading—the first poem to engage and the following ones to take the reader on an emotional or intellectual ride. You don't want to put a real serious poem, say about the Holocaust, next to a funny one. Right? Of course, some people organize a book by themes—nature poems, family poems, love poems, etc. Sometimes that works, but for the most part it's overdone and sort of boring, there being no surprises.

All I can do is tell you how *I* organize a book. I imagine every poet does it differently and you'll have to figure out what works for you. One of my early books, **Inverted Fire**, was organized this way: I had just had a poem I especially liked, "Stars," picked up by *Poetry*, so I wanted to open the book with that poem. The poem begins with a quote:

> Heraclitus said
> *stars are bowls of inverted fire*

So, after much thinking, I came around to the idea of dividing the book into sections, each one having something to do with astronomy and the night sky. What I ended up with was four sections: Libra, which contains the personal poems since Libra is my sign; The Moon, which contains poems touching on more thoughtful, serene themes; Black Hole, which contains the very darkest pieces; and finally, Red Shift, which lifts, and indeed shifts, the overarching arc (which is astronomy) from the despondent pieces of Black Hole to end the book on a defiantly upbeat note. Here's the final poem so you can see what I mean.

Night Drive

Tonight the trees are tossing the clouds around
and the moon in her wedge of white make-up
leans back to hold us in her spotlight of hair.
A dog barks. A garage door lowers and locks.
And every building freezes for the portrait of the world.

Where is defeat on such a night as this?
Each pebble on the side of the road
shouts a victory in the flash of my headlights,
for I have come to the end of fifty-five years,
each one the eraser for the last, each one
a newly sharpened pencil jabbing me awake
to this picture—here and hung—on this night's black wall.

And I am driving, driving for Jimmy Wonderland
down the white line of my own intentions,
glancing in the rear-view mirror with a stone's cold eye.
And I know I have never been here before
for I've thrown the old key out the car window to lie
in a ditch somewhere in a broken spill of trash—crockery,

egg shells, an unloved dolly clutching at the dirt.
Imagine what you like: say this film
is a loop played round and before, or that I drive
a winding hill passing the same sign on repeated rights.
But it is night. The dark surrounds, presses, then
slides off. I *see* no sign but this white immediacy
quickening in the brights of my car. And nowhere
beyond the reach of my eyes is more sweet than here
when marrow blooms in the bone and starts to speak.

It's important to end a book with a strong poem, a sort of statement that says where you want to leave your reader. If you have troubles organizing a book—a very difficult project that may take not just weeks, but months—I suggest that you look at the way other poets have done it and see what appeals to you. Look at your favorite writers and study the different ways an organization is carried out. There are many possibilities. And good luck!

Specialty books are those that do not easily fit into one of the typical book genres. They are typically targeted to a narrow market niche with a unique interest. They include photography books, cookbooks, travel books, how-to books, coffee table books, self-help books, prayer books, comic books, journals and guides. We have chosen two types of specialty books—coffee table books and cookbooks—for tips and techniques.

Chapter 15
How to Write
A Specialty Book:
Coffee Table Books
By Gail Vail

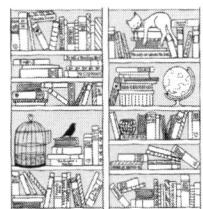

"An art book is a museum without walls."

—Andre Malraux

My eureka moment struck in late 2008. As a frequent guest to the local writers' guild and an active member of the local art community, I listened to stories and poems and visualized paintings that paired with the writings. It dawned on me that a collaboration would make a beautiful, illustrated coffee table book for the Lake Oconee area. Coffee table books are best crafted around principles. Here are a few and how they were applied to my coffee table book.

Follow your passion. What do you want on your coffee table? No doubt a book that can be picked up and appreciated instantly. Perhaps a book that relates to a hobby or an area where you once lived but at a minimum one that covers a topic of keen interest.

Decide on a theme. To make this book appealing to potential buyers, I decided to include stories, poems and paintings as a reflection of various aspects of life at Lake Oconee. Organized by seasons, the book began with spring, the season of rebirth and growth, and ended with winter, a season serene and beautiful in its own way.

Use diverse content. After collecting, sorting and retaining relevant writings, I contacted artists who had paintings closely aligned with the writings. Some stories needed new paintings and some paintings needed new writings—no problem for the local talent.

Organize with a deliberate rhythm. Time was spent sequencing stories with poems, interspersing longer pieces with shorter ones, and mixing humorous with serious. The paintings were chosen not to overtly illustrate but to relate to the writings in a way they would bring added pleasure to the reader.

Choose a format. With the help of a local graphic designer, we decided to keep the book small, resulting in a 6½ x 9½" hardcover book with a colorful dust jacket. Each left page included prose or poem with each right facing page featuring a painting. The 88-page book included the works of 23 area writers and 20 area artists.

Focus on the details. The process was complex as writings needed to be edited for content and length to fit the allotted space. Content had to be sorted into the appropriate season. Some new topics needed to be covered to complete the perspective on lake life. Releases needed to be signed and other little details addressed to yield a successful publication.

The resulting book, **Seasons on Lake Oconee**, proved popular in the area and spurred a local talented writer to proceed with two more hardcover books of his writings, illustrated with full color paintings by area artists (**The Seasonal Heart** and **Turning Leaves** by George Heiring and Gail Vail).

A coffee table book needs to look classy and be catchy to the eye, no matter the subject. Size is less of an issue, although in an era of downsizing, smaller may be more appealing. Coffee table books, unlike novels, can be picked up and read in bits and in any order, while lingering over coffee or perhaps a glass of fine wine. What's on your coffee table?

Chapter 16

How to Write a Specialty Book: Cookbooks

By Derin Moore, CMC

"Good food is like music you can taste, color you can smell.
There is excellence all around you.
You need only to be aware to stop and savor it."
—Chef Anguste Gusteau, *Ratatouille*

The Academy Award winning movie **Ratatouille** is my favorite cooking movie. The features that made this film a hit are the characteristics that make cookbooks successful. **Ratatouille** was delightfully unique, creatively novel, with impeccable accuracy. The animated actors' movements were the exact motions of great chefs. The layout of the Paris kitchen and style of old French chefs were precise. And, the movie appealed to master chefs as well as young children. Crafting a winning cookbook requires a few critical success factors.

Begin with Rapport. Cooking can be intimidating, its end result embarrassing. Start your kinship with your reader by warmly outlining your principles. "We always use whole milk, real butter, Heinz vinegar, etc." You won't have to repeat this same guidance throughout. Outline how your recipes will be structured and your distinctive, adventuresome way of covering key elements. Avoid arrogance; provide encouragement. Connect like a friend.

Make Your Cookbook Inspirational. Cookbooks that endure inspire as much as they instruct. Inspiration occurs if the book has a sense of soul, not just a list of directions. It must be distinctive in presentation, accurate in direction, and thought-provoking in substance. Make it approachable, accessible, intriguing, with recipes created around ingredients readily available. Never lose sight of "What would make my mom want to buy this book?"

Choose an Organizing Structure. Create a "go to" cookbook buyers will want to leave out on the counter, not just bring out on special occasions. Recipes should be presented in order of use but with early warnings like "first, melt the butter" or "preheat the oven." Facilitate discipline and efficiency in preparation through steps that can occur simultaneously. Arrange for easy, quick access, including a strong index. Paint a clear picture of the final product. Use measurements, terminology, and pack sizes easily understood and consistent throughout the book.

Add a Bit of Novelty. Whimsy leaves readers less intimidated. Novelty could be a cartoon with speech bubbles that provide gentle warnings. It might be recipe alternatives appealing to the most advanced reader. It could be catchy recipe titles. Bottom line, it should leave some content to a reader's imagination, leading him or her in content and direction to a final product that produces fun and interest.

Test, and Test Again. Pay close attention to your use of proper weights, measures, scales and oven thermometer. A true test is only done by an amateur using your recipe for the first time. Again, your mom is a great quality-control guide for the work-ability and practicality of your recipes.

Provide Head Notes. Headnotes provide backstories behind recipes. They might provide a bit of history or legend. They entertain while enriching the reader's understanding. Always include a healthy serving of "why" before "what and how." Make headnotes creatively lure readers into wanting to know more. Make maximum use of visuals. Connect your reader to your passion and experience. It sounds like, "The following recipe is near and dear to my heart, and the memories and history of the dish were created by my great-grandmother of German decent who taught me this summer after summer while I was growing up."

"Chefs think about what it's like to make food. Being a scientist in the kitchen is about asking why something works, and how it works," wrote Chef Nathan Myhrvold. His quote is a reminder that a great cookbook should educate as it entertains, inspires as it instructs. Make your writing as savory as your topic.

Chapter 17
How to Get a Book Published

"If Moses were alive today he'd come down from the mountain with the Ten Commandments and spend the next five years trying to get them published."
—Anonymous

After a long losing streak, coaching great Vince Lombardi gathered together his Green Bay Packers professional football team in the middle of the field and said, "We need to start with the basics." Holding up one of the practice balls he announced, "Gentlemen, *this* is a football!" The team went on to win three NFL championships and two Super Bowls. With every endeavor, the basics and fundamentals matter.

Publishing is the crafting of a large collection of words assembled in a fashion that can be made available to be read and/

or purchased by the public. Books do not have to be in forms that can be placed on a shelf in the library or bookstore; today they can be an electronic version viewed on a computer or electronic device. But, they are not considered published until they are made available in some readable form for public consumption.

Getting your book from your computer or writing pad to the public is the role of a publisher. Today, there are three forms of publishing: a traditional publisher, self-publishing, and a hybrid form of the two. In this chapter, we will examine the pros and cons of each as well as offer tips about ways to make each form work for you. Your decision on the best form of publishing will largely depend on money, time, and your desire for control.

Using a Traditional Publisher

Only about 30% of books published today use a traditional publisher. That is because the traditional publisher typically provides all the funding necessary to publish a book and is therefore interested in accepting only books likely to sell to the book's target market. Keep these stark statistics in mind, not to be discouraged but to appreciate the realities of book marketing. The average non-fiction book published today (traditional and self-publishing combined) earns less than $250 in its first year and less than $2000 over its lifetime. Of the million or so books published each year, there is less than a 1% chance of a book's being stocked in a bookstore.[32]

Now, for the hard-to-hear news. Your royalty is likely to be only 15% of the revenue generated by the publisher. That means if your book is sold on Amazon, it likely will be sold at a 25 to 30% discount from the list price plus their 15-20% profit. So, a $20 list price book is really a $10 book to your publisher, which means your royalty will be about $1.50 per book; fifty cents (or 5%) if your book is sold internationally. Don't get discouraged; it can still be well worth the effort!

Given these incredible odds, your chance of getting a publisher to love your book depends on a great book proposal. The book proposal is to a book what a resume is to a job applicant and more. For most non-fiction books, you do not have to have finished writing the book to land a book contract. For novels, you will need to send the entire book. Don't approach a book agent or editor until it is your very best final version. There are lots of great resources on the Internet and in our resource section about writing a great book proposal. Here are the basics:

Cover letter: This is your sampler to get a book agent (we will get to them in a minute) or the acquisition editor for the publisher to even read your proposal. It is no more than one page. Assume the reader gets fifty proposals a day. If the agent (or publisher) is not intrigued in the first couple of paragraphs, he or she is not likely to spend time reading any more. Make it short, clever, punchy and authentic. Let the reader know quickly your "big idea" for the book and why it will be important to your target audience. Outline your target audience and your personal connection with your topic as well as your qualifications to deliver this unique message through your book. You should also communicate the anticipated book length and target date for completion of your manuscript.

Overview of the Book: This section communicates in more detail your big idea along with your view of how your target market will benefit from your book. Ray Bard, CEO of Bard Books, says, "You need to communicate precisely what you are selling—information, hope, results or pleasure; and is your message aligned and fresh. Does it have a sizzle and a snap?" You need to be convincing that you know your target market and a few hints about how you plan to market your book. Remember, you are asking a publisher to make a sizable financial investment. If the publisher sees no market for your book, the publisher will turn it down no matter how well your book might be written. Publishers are not looking for great books, they are interested only in great books that will sell. The overview should be no more than two pages.

Author Bio: This is not just a typical biographical sketch; it should communicate the reasons you are the best person on the planet to write this particular book. It should reference your platform (See the "How to Market a New Book" chapter) and your network. Keep this in mind. Unless you are already a famous author, you will be the primary salesperson for your book. The publisher will need to be convinced you can sell a lot of copies of your book through your self-generated publicity. This fact cannot be overstated. Your book sales will be critically anchored to your network and your ability to influence your marketplace.

Target Audience: The primary market is the main audience for your book. However, do not forget secondary audiences like libraries, associations, or people in professions associated with your subject. If you wrote a murder mystery, your secondary audience might be people in law enforcement or forensics. Include as many audiences as you can.

Book Competition: This is not the place to say there is no other book quite like yours! Think of your competition as the titles your target audience might buy instead of yours, or ones they may already have purchased similar to yours. Be thorough; the more comprehensive your list, the more you convince an agent or acquisitions editor that you know your marketplace.

Table of Contents: While the agent or editor knows this is likely to change if you are still writing the book, it can reveal the breadth of the book and the "storyline" it seeks to follow.

Sample Chapter: If you have written several chapters and this is a non-fiction book, select your best. Do not submit the first chapter since it is less likely to be a typical "working" chapter. Some non-fiction writers send the first chapter as well as a working chapter. The challenge is this: the more content you send, the less likely it will be read...unless, it is super compelling. If it is fiction, you will need to send the entire book.

One important consideration is whether to send your book proposal directly to the publisher (typically the acquisition editor) or use a book or literary agent. Agents know the publishers and the kinds of books they will accept. About 80% of the books published by the large New York publishers are sold by an agent. If an agent likes your proposal, she or he will help you improve your book proposal and will shop it to publishers. For this service, they typically take 15% of any advance and royalties. Avoid agents that charge fees. If your book is published, royalty checks will go to your agent. Your agent will keep her or his commission and send you the balance. We have included a section on book agents in the "With a Little Help from Friends" chapter.

Self-Publishing

One of the best books around on how to self-publish is **APE** (authors, publishers and editors) found in the resources section. The main advantage to self-publishing is you get the exact book you want. You can also bring the book out much faster (traditional book publishers can take 18 months to bring your book out once you sign the contract). It is a bit like buying a house versus building one when you are the general contractor. For self-publishing, you are funding the entire operation; you also get to keep all the revenue, minus your expense for bringing the book to market! Self-publishing can be less frustrating than traditional publishing if you assemble the right team. But, remember, you need to create a distribution process, something traditional publishers already have.

Here is a typical sequence if you considered it in a linear fashion. Obviously, some of these steps could happen simultaneously. You write the book and hire an editor. There are four types. There is a manuscript development editor who can help brainstorm what the book is, who it is for, how it will be different, and can then develop and provide feedback during the writing process. There is an editor we will call a vernacular engineer.

This is an editor who works on the structure of the book, often rearranging paragraphs, suggesting sections be rewritten, tightened, lengthened, etc. The third type is the typical editor who is much like a grammar teacher looking at syntax, grammar infractions, suggesting alternative words or phrases to make your work smoother and an easier read for your target audience. The fourth type of editor is a copyeditor who prepares your finished manuscript for book design and ultimately for printing.

Your book is now ready for a designer, who does book layout and interior design, essentially getting your book ready to go to the printer, assuming it is a physical book and not an e-book. Cover designers craft a book cover that is the eye-catching "advertising" message to your buyer to take a closer look at your book. Your book now goes to a printer, who turns it into a product that can be inventoried, marketing, purchased, and distributed. You are now ready to market your new book. Marketing is covered in the next chapter; the business side of authoring—contracts, distribution agreements, audio and foreign rights, publicists, etc. will be covered in a later chapter.

Knowing the mechanics of how to get published is for naught if your book is not well written and one of interest to your target market. Keep in mind, some books start off as self-published, grow a huge following, and end up with a traditional publisher.

Hybrid Publishing

Hybrid publishers are much like traditional publisher except you fund it completely and they take care of all the details from editing to marketing to distribution. They take on the General Contractor role, to continue our earlier house-building analogy. All hybrid publishers are not alike, so do your homework. Some have retail distribution and produce very high-quality books; others do not. Many hybrid publishers provide a writer with a sort of Chinese menu enabling you to select the features you want to pay them to perform, leaving the rest to you. For example, you might want a hybrid publisher to produce, print and then ship you the inventory, which you warehouse, market, and distribute. Authors choosing this approach typically have their own marketing and shipping resources. You might want to read Tanya Hall's book **Ideas, Influence and Income**.

...And They Said "No"

Rejection letters are tough. You pour your heart and soul into a manuscript only to have it shunned by an acquisitions editor. Brood awhile, bathe in your disappointment, share your sorrow with a friend, and then get back up and go forward again. Every book is not right for every publisher at every time. And, you are in the company of other great writers who shared your setback.

We started with the dark side of getting published. But, we end with a note of encouragement. Mystery writer, Agatha Christie kept sending her first book to editors for five years until it was finally accepted. She has sold over two billion dollars' worth of books. Children's author Dr. Seuss was told his first book, **And I think I Saw It on Mulberry Street**, was "too different from other juveniles on market to warrant its selling." He did not give up; he is today the ninth best-selling fiction author of all time. Western writer Zane Grey was told: "You have no business being a writer and should give up." He went on to sell 250 million books! Alice Walker's **The Color Purple** was rejected with the criticism that she used too many exclamation points. It went on to sell ten million copies and win both the Pulitzer Prize and the National Book Award for fiction.

One final story of encouragement. When the biggest selling author of this century, J. K. Rowling, wrote her first Harry Potter book, twelve publishing houses turned it down. When Bloomsbury finally agreed to publish her book, it came with a note advising her to "get a day job." She didn't. She kept writing. Today, she is the ninth biggest selling author of all time and worth almost a billion dollars. Don't give up!

Chapter 18
How to Market A New Book

"If writing and publishing a book is like giving birth to a child, then book marketing is like rearing it."
—Heather Hart

Ralph Waldo Emerson was wrong! Now, before we get in hot water with teachers of American literature, let's set the record straight. Ralph was often misquoted. He never mentioned anything about a better mousetrap. What he actually said was, "If a man has good corn or wood, or boards, or pigs, to sell, or can make better chairs or knives, crucibles or church organs, than anybody else, you will find a broad hard-beaten road to his house, though it be in the woods."[33] Emerson was still dead wrong!

In Emerson's day in the mid-1800s, people's lives revolved largely around a small village. Everyone pretty much knew everyone within miles. And, the gossip started at the local pub or blacksmith shop could easily reach the ears of about everyone within a day. Today, no matter how great your book happens to be, if your marketplace does not know about it, not even a few people will beat a path to your door. You have to become a perpetual, hard-working marketer of your new book.

Social Media Is Social

Today, book selling starts with the Internet and social media. All social gatherings have manners. When you go to a party you know you are supposed to have fun but not start any fights. Manners are especially true for social media—especially since it can be anonymous. Tara Hunt, author of **The Whuffie Factor**, put it this way: "Whuffie," she wrote, "is the residual outcome—the currency—of your reputation. You lose or gain it based on positive and negative actions, your contribution to the community. Influence comes through being nice, being networked, and being notable. There is no room for bullies with lots of money. Money may buy you an audience but it will not guarantee influence."[34]

Create a Buzz

Marketing your new book starts long before you finish writing it. It starts with clearly identifying your target market—the main folks likely to be interested in your book topic. Think about where your target audience goes, what they read, what websites they likely visit, the people they are likely to know. Brainstorm ways to get your book (or excerpts from your book) in front of them. Pull out short teaser chapters and find ways to place them in newspapers, send them to magazines or blog sites likely read by your audience.

Speak at conferences attended by your target audience as well as before civic and church groups. Always use a handout that includes information about and/or from your new book. Make certain your teasers have the words, "Adapted from the forthcoming book..." at the end. If you have a business card, put a photo of the book cover on the back. It is not about being a shameless marketer; it is about honoring the special gift the universe has bestowed upon you to share with others.

One buzz-building aspect is the titling of your book. Most traditional publishers have the final say on a book title but would never select a title you did not like since you are the primary salesperson for the book. With self-publishing and hybrid publishing you have total control over your title but hopefully with wise input from professionals who know the book market. Titles need to have two features: clarity and attraction. Clarity helps buyers know a bit about what they are buying. A compelling title with a sense of intrigue helps create a buzz and reinforces your brand. Many authors let the subtitle of their book carry the clarity load. Remember, book titling is about marketing more than anything. It is the same as an object- making company branding the name of a new product.

Build a Platform

A platform is your brand communication in your marketplace. It tells your market who you are and what you are about. It reflects your vision or noble purpose. And, your book is obviously a part of that. Your platform might include a website where potential book buyers can come and learn about your book, perhaps even order a copy. Write a regular blog for your website which gives readers a reason to come back. Make sure your name at the end of all your emails mentions your website address and information about your book, right along with your email address. Make sure your contact information is at the end of your book.

Consider getting a memorable email address (called a vanity URL) instead of a Gmail or Yahoo domain address. JohnG@gmail.com is not a promotional email address. However, john@johngrisham.com carries a totally different message. Once you have your own domain (from GoDaddy or Web.com), you can build an inexpensive website. Drive traffic to your website by including it with everything you make public. Create a short newsletter that goes to your email list. It makes your readers feel they are important.

Grow a Network

Your network includes people who will not only buy your book but will recommend it to friends. So, how do you grow a network? Do book readings. Get on local media. Get on social media networks like Facebook, Twitter, Google+ and LinkedIn. Reach out to others to invite them to join you on these networks. Send out content to your followers regularly. Some authors, for example, send out tweets several times a day. There are programs like Buffer, Sprout Social, and Hootsuite that enable you to plan scores of tweets (now up to 280 characters each) and blogs in advance, programming them to appear precisely when you elect. TweetDeck is just for scheduling and monitoring tweets. Add a ClickToTweet link to your blog posts to make it easy for others to share.

Do author visits either live or via Skype or Zoom. Set up your own YouTube channel and post short videos about your book. These are simple to do with your smartphone. You can purchase boom microphones that attach to the bottom of your smartphone to give you clear sound for shooting videos in a noisy setting. There are inexpensive apps (like Wondershare Filmora and Apple Final Cut Pro) that enable you to easily edit your videos. You can include them in your e-newsletters and send them out as e-blasts to your email list or Twitter followers.

Help other authors be successful. When you get a tweet, retweet it to your network. When you read a blog that you like, send it to your followers. Remember Tara Hunt's advice to "be kind, networked and notable." By growing your following, you are in a position to borrow other's network by asking them to post a guest blog on their website. Give away books, especially to those who can help promote, review or encourage others to purchase your new book. There are more tools than we have space to mention, but key ones to learn more about are Feedly, HARO, ProfNet, Hashtags, StumbleUpon, Pinterest, Get Abstract, Net Galley, RSS Feeds, etc.

Solicit Endorsements and Reviews

Reviews start with endorsements. Endorsements on the cover of your book signal that influential people have found it to be useful or valuable. It is essentially a product review. Select people for endorsements your target audience will either know, or know the organization they lead. Getting an endorsement from your preacher might be nice, but unless your preacher is Joel Osteen, it might not have the influence you need. Be careful of endorsements from controversial people. Your endorsement from the Republican governor might not carry much weight if your target audience happens to be largely Democrat! Once your book is out, reviews are central to communicating to your marketplace that someone should buy your book. Again, select people whom your target market respects, send them a complimentary copy of your book, and request that they write a short review on your book on Amazon, B&N.com and Goodreads. We have included a section on endorsers and reviewers in the "With a Little Help from Friends" chapter.

Produce a Media or Press Kit

Calling up the local radio or television station and asking to be interviewed about your new book will not likely work unless the host happens to be your second cousin! You will need a great media or press kit to pitch radio, television, newspapers, and even power bloggers, those individuals who have huge online networks. If your media kit is mailed, it needs to be in a great-looking color folder with inside sleeves on both sides. You can purchase them at any stationery store.

What goes in the sleeves? You will need a high-quality color head shot, a 100-150-word biography, a one sheet for your book—that is, a single piece of paper that shows a color photo of the book cover, a description of the book (a two-paragraph summary), a half-dozen questions with answers about the book, a few key endorsements. Also, include a dozen questions an interviewer can use should you get on her or his show. If you have had other media events (radio, television or print) include them. Make certain you have correct contact information. If your media kit is sent electronically, it needs to contain the same information. Then, write your 30- second elevator speech about what your book is about and practice it until you can recite it in your sleep. Should a reporter call you to conduct a preliminary interview to determine if you would be right for the show, you will sound confident and poised.

Media Pitches

Media pitches are in the same nature as media kits but crafted to target a reviewer, reporter, or producer. Let's say you want to land a five-minute spot on a TV news program or get quoted in an article in a major magazine. "Go to school" on the reporter, producer or columnist so you can reference your admiration for their work. Give them enough about your book to be a tease, not a full description. Find an obvious hook that sets you apart. And, be sure to telegraph your unique expertise on this specific topic. Keep your pitch to about 500 words. Reporters, reviewers and producers get many pitches; yours needs to be short and catchy.

Young Al Hopkins watched his friends every summer set up a lemonade stand on a street corner in his small hometown and wait for a passerby to make a sale. He decided there was a better way. On Friday afternoon, he delivered to every house in town a flyer promising "amazing blue lemonade coming to your door on Saturday." Saturday morning, he loaded up his red wagon with blue-colored lemonade his mom helped him make and went door-to-door knocking on doors. He made enough money that summer to buy a Schwinn bicycle with a light and a bell. Make your book unique and take it "on the road" instead of waiting on a street corner hoping for a sale!

Chapter 19

With a Little Help from Friends

"No author dislikes to be edited as much as he dislikes not to be published."

—J. Russell Lynes

Writing is a solo experience—just you and the pen or keyboard. But, authoring is a collaborative effort. You can write it alone; you cannot sell it alone…at least, not very well. Collaborative literally means "to labor together." In this chapter, we will explore some of the potential members of your authoring team with whom you are likely to be laboring. You might not need them all; you will clearly need some of them. They will be introduced somewhat in the order you are likely to need them. We start with one you will need throughout the writing process.

Cheerleaders

"No compulsion in the world is stronger than the urge to edit someone else's document," wrote famous science fiction writer H. G. Wells.[35] His quote signals how easy it is for us all to give our opinions or advice. As a writer, you will benefit from affirmations as you write, feedback as you edit. Criticizing a writer's work is as offensive to them as commenting on someone's ugly baby! Providing help that is actually helpful can be a delicate but doable task. Tell your cheerleaders precisely what you need. Provide a context. This sounds like: "I am working on this chapter of my new book and it would be a great to let me know what you like about it. I will be back to you later on to get your feedback and critique."

When it comes time for feedback, after the first draft of the book has been completed, provide your cheerleaders with a few ground rules for providing critique. Unless your friend is a writer, steer the feedback toward the perspective of a reader. Musicians don't ask non-musicians to critique their chord construction! It sounds like this: "If you were a reader of this book, what do you think works, doesn't work, is unclear, is interesting, is boring? How does the book make you feel?" Again, focus your cheerleader only on what she or he is best qualified to critique." If your cheerleader has a tendency to be negative you might need to coach, "So, what did you like most about my book?"

Editors

Editors are generally involved after the first draft of your book has been completed. In an earlier chapter, we described four types of editors—a developmental editor, a vernacular engineer (or structural editor), a traditional editor, and a copyeditor. While it is not helpful to bias an editor as he or she prepares to focus on your book, it is helpful to be crystal clear on your expectations. Communicate your goals for the book and your hopes regarding how it will impact or influence your target audience. One of the objectives of a good editor is to prepare your manuscript to be the best it can be in achieving your unique book goals.

Let your editor(s) know the unique writing style you want the book to reflect. Editors refer to it as "your voice." It means the book needs to sound like you and read like you wrote it. Heavy-handed editors can sometimes edit the book so it reads like they wrote it. Editors are not ghost writers, crafting a book on your behalf; they are polishers of your unique creation. The more detail you can provide about the spirit and tone of your book, the better the editor will be at retaining "your voice." Sometimes writers want to use a particular approach to communication— one-word sentences, one-sentence paragraphs, made-up words, odd layouts—approaches that might frustrate your high school English teacher. Communicate your preference to the editor so he or she does not "alter" what is signature you.

Agents

Book or literary agents are essentially book brokers. They are to a book what a realtor is to a house. They take a commission for successfully pitching your book to a traditional book publisher. We provided an overview of their role earlier. Look for someone who specializes in your genre. Most agents have a website and highlight books they have previously sold. Does their cadre of success stories match your type of book? If not, look elsewhere. Assuming it does and you like what they promote, call authors of books they have represented to learn of their experiences. Since this person is the individual who stands between your manuscript and your book in the bookstore window, pick the best match. There are many book agents listed on WritersMarket.com, AgentQuery.com and PublisherMarketplace.com.

Book agents have three basic roles—to find you a publisher, to get you as large an advance as possible, and to negotiate the best terms for your publishing contract. Given the economic challenges of most publishing companies today, unless you are someone likely to give them a runaway best-seller, advances are unlikely. Advances are simply paying some of your royalties up front. A $10,000 advance means you will get a check (less the 15% your book agent takes), and then receive no royalties until your book earns what would have been $10,000 in royalties. Even with a good book agent, it is advisable to have your attorney review your book contract before you sign it. We will explore the business side of authoring in a later chapter.

Endorsers

Endorsements can provide important power to the marketability of your book. Endorsements are usually placed on the back cover or in the first few pages of the book. A really important one might go on the front cover. The number of endorsements is not as important as the influence of the endorsers. Getting influential endorsers starts with having a great book. When you send a potential endorser a draft of your manuscript, it needs to look its best; but more importantly, it needs to be your best work. Suggest their endorsement be short (1 or 2 sentences) since brief remarks are more likely to be read by a prospective buyer.

It is not necessary that you personally know the endorser, but rather that you have a way to network to that person. It may require a bit of sleuth work, likely done on the Internet. Let's say you want an endorsement from *Forbes* editor-in-chief, Steve Forbes. You learn on the Internet that Steve graduated from a particular college in California, a class ahead of the former CEO of Home Depot. The former CEO's wife is a senior leader for Habitat for Humanity. You have a good friend who is very active with Habitat. You might ask your friend to connect with the former CEO's wife about your new book. You speculate she knows Steve and might be willing to approach Steve…etc. If there is an indication of a willingness to endorse your book, it is sometimes helpful to write a couple of straw endorsements for the endorser to use, edit, or just employ as a guide.

Publicists

Publicists are professional book promoters. Good publicists know social media (on the Internet) and traditional media (radio, TV, newspaper, etc.). They can craft and submit media pitches to get your book mentioned. They can talk with reporters and producers on your behalf to land you an appearance on a traditional media outlet. Some book publicists will manage the publicity side of your platform, including writing and posting tweets, hosting webinars and podcasts. They can set up and manage book signings. They ensure your book is properly and effectively presented on book-selling websites like Amazon, BN.com, etc. Some coach you on a myriad of ways to promote your book. Some have webmasters who build book promotion components for your website. Some help manage your website SEO (search engine optimization) so your book is positioned high (i.e., early) on the pages of the major search engines (like Google, Bing and Yahoo).

There are pros and cons for using book publicists. If your goal is selling a lot of books, a book launch can be complex and frustrating. Turning it over to a publicist can free you to focus on other priorities. Being experienced PR pros, they likely know avenues for book marketing you might miss. Being always in the marketplace, they can spot trends, angles, and approaches and respond quickly to unique opportunities. The downside is the fact that the pursuit of effective publicity that translates into book sales is a leap of faith. While some publicists are "pay for play," meaning you only pay for the publicity hits you get, there is no guarantee that getting a live appearance on Oprah will actually translate into more books sold.

Reviewers

Reviewers come in many forms. Some reviewers review books for magazines or blogs. Some review them on major book sites like Amazon, Goodreads, BN.com, and 800CEORead.com. Reviewers, like endorsers, signal to readers that your book warranted their esteem. They are like references on a resume, likes on Facebook, or mentions on Yelp. Some reviews come indirectly from your marketing and publicity; someone heard about your book, read it, and posted a review.

Don't wait for unsolicited reviews. Send your book to lots of friends and request they review it on your behalf. Reviewing books on major book selling sites is easy and fast. Again, as with endorsements, you can even provide them a couple of examples. You will also want to ask the people who wrote endorsements for your book cover to post them as reviews on book-selling sites.

The romantic view of a solitary writer pounding the keys and only communicating with some editor in New York is just that—romantic and unrealistic. Success in the book world today comes with connection. And, being linked to social friends who can cheer you on and specialist friends who can enhance the quality and reach of your work is vital to helping your book maximize its potential.

In the movie **Ratatouille**, the main character aspires to be a great chef. He periodically gets encouragement from the imaginary chef named Auguste Gusteau who once owned and ran a famous restaurant in Paris. His words could have been for writers aspiring to be authors as well.

"You must be imaginative, strong-hearted. You must try things that may not work, and you must not let anyone define your limits because of where you come from. Your only limit is your soul. What I say is true, anyone can cook...but only the fearless can be great."[36]

Chapter 20

The Business Side Of Authoring

"To produce a mighty book,
you must choose a mighty theme."
—Herman Melville

"Life is like a box of chocolates, you never know what you're gonna get."[37] It was one of the most memorable lines from the hit movie **Forrest Gump**. It could have been the theme for Winston Groom, the author of the book on which the movie was based. In this case, he may have gotten poor advice on the business of authoring and wound up with a "bitter tasting chocolate."

Here are the facts. **Forrest Gump** was the highest grossing film in 1994, earning over $677 million.[38] It won six Academy Awards including best picture, best director and best actor.

Groom negotiated with Paramount Pictures to be paid $350,000 plus 3% of the film's net profits for the screenplay rights to his book. Want to guess how much Groom actually received? Zero. Tom Hanks, the best actor award winner for the film, negotiated a contract to take no salary but instead a percentage of the film's gross receipts. He earned $40 million for the movie.

Hollywood accounting legally inflated the expenses of the film to show an eighty million-dollar paper loss to maximize profit sharing. Studio accounting, for example, allowed a movie company to take a portion of revenue and set it aside as a provision for future bad movies. Groom was an expense. A contract based on net profits, as Groom's contract was, got nothing; one based on gross receipts, as Hanks' contract was, was handsomely rewarded.

When Groom took Paramount Pictures to court, according to accounting professor Aswath Damadaron, the case lasted 15 minutes. In testimony, the judge said to Groom, "So basically you put your faith in the hands of their accountant. Is that right?" Groom replied, "I guess so." The judge continued, "The case is dismissed. You got what you deserved."[39]

In this chapter, we examine some of the main business components important to authoring. The bottom line is this: when you are negotiating the business side of authoring, the old adage from author Jean Shephard might be good advice: "In God we trust: all others pay cash."[40] It is not that the people with whom you are likely dealing are malicious or unscrupulous. As in Paramount

Pictures' dealings with Winston Groom, their interests are first and foremost their own welfare.

Book Contracts

You get the thrilling news a publisher has accepted your manuscript and would like to publish it. With the news comes a standard book contract. Stop!! Do not reach for that pen to sign! Study the contract carefully; get an attorney to review it, preferably a publishing or intellectual property attorney. If you do not have access to a publishing lawyer, read a good book on publishing law. There are two in the resource section.

Never give up the copyright of your book and make certain the contract contains language to that fact. Include a clause requiring the publisher to register your copyright with the U.S. Copyright Office within 90 days of the date of publication. Other ways to protect your work include nixing any clause that gives the publisher license to change your manuscript in any way without your approval.

Do not allow the publisher to tie up your work. Publishers have been known to agree to publish your book, drag their feet for months and months, and then elect to not publish it. Insist on a publication deadline, and if it is not honored, end the agreement. Watch out for a clause that gives the publisher rights to any "competing works." This is a tool a publisher uses to get first refusal on your next book. If you have a negative experience with a publisher, the last thing you want to do is do another book with them. And, never forget there are predator publishers. Www.

predatoryjournals.com is worth checking to avoid ending up with a publisher that preys on new authors eager to publish their work.

Line Extensions

Line extensions are other forms your book might take. All publishers today will want a print version and an e-print version of your book since many customers are reading books on an e-reader (like Nook,® Kindle,® or IPad®). Publishers seek rights to publish your book in another language expanding your reach to new markets. These are fine, but be very careful. What if the back cover of your book published in Hungary in Hungarian includes photos of other books published by that foreign publisher, and one is pornographic, something legal in that country?

The publisher will likely also want all line extensions. Do not give them away. Line extensions could be an audio version of your book. Your book might be one a film producer would like to turn into a movie. Training companies sometimes want to create a training program based on your book. This list of line extensions is…well, extensive! The primary issues are control and integrity.

Let's take a training company, for example. Your publisher cuts a deal with a training company to turn your book into a training program for which you are paid a commission based on their sales. Even if the deal is financially a good one, the integrity of your work is in the hands of practitioners over whom you have no control. What if the trainer who teaches your content is mediocre or poor? It reflects on you and your brand. What if the movie based on your book bombs at the box office?

Control can only occur if you use extreme caution in the contract phase. Remember the opening story. Line extension companies will write a contract that favors their interests before yours, that will seek their control over yours. The more cautious eyes you can get to review your agreement, especially an intellectual property attorney, the more likely you are to catch a tiny loophole you could later regret. Just because you are a new, inexperienced author does not mean you should sell out your integrity, even if it results in your having a best-seller.

Copyrights, Permissions and Protections

Copyright is a smart legal device to protect your work from being misused or claimed by others. When seeking a copyright from the U. S. Copyright Office (a part of the Library of Congress), your goal today should be to obtain world rights, not just U.S. rights. Imagine your book being a runaway hit in Canada by a different author because your copyright protection only covered use in the U.S. Also, remember you cannot copyright an idea or even a book title. You copyright a particular collection of words.

This brings us to another vital principle. Your book should contain only your original work. If you borrow quotes from others, you must give that writer credit in a footnote or endnote. If you borrow several sentences (like a paragraph), you will need written permission from its author plus a footnote. Use primary sources, not secondary sources for cites or footnotes. If you saw a quote by someone in an article written by someone else, go to the original location where the quote appeared. This might take some research on your part, but it is far better than having to defend your "fair use" of the quote in a court of law.

Permission to use cartoons, lyrics from songs, or photos done by others typically requires written permission and often a fee. Just because you found a great photo on Google Images does not mean you have the right to use it in a book you are claiming to be yours. There are image shops on the Internet that offer royalty-free graphics (like shutterstock.com, iphotostock.com, 123RF.com, or gettyimage.com). Royalty-free means you do not have to pay a fee for each book in which the image appears; it does mean you have to pay a fee to use the photo. It also means you must credit the creator of the image.

Helpers

We covered helpers in the chapter called "With a Little Help from Friends." In this chapter, we examine a few cautions about the darker side of helpers—specifically those with whom you have a fiduciary relationship. As mentioned earlier, hiring a book or literary agent to shop and pitch your book to a publisher on your behalf will generally cost you 15% of your advance and royalties. If you are a brand-new author, it can be well worth the investment. Here are a few cautions:

Watch out for any requests for fees upfront. There are agents who will want a "reading fee" or "signing fee." Most good book agents do not charge any up-front fee but instead take their commission from the checks the publisher would send to you directly had the agent not been the go-between. And, your royalty checks should come with a complete accounting of copies sold and royalties earned. Make certain your agent only represents one book at a time. Be crystal clear on when your relationship comes to an end. As earlier mentioned, think of agents much like a real estate agent. If you contracted a real estate agent to sell your house and you had no house showings in six months, you might want to find a different agent. The same is true for book agents.

Publicity agent warnings are similar. PR firms are hired by the author to promote a book to traditional and social media. Their work typically starts 60 to 90 days before a new book launches and continues 60 to 90 days afterward. Hiring a PR firm is a "leap of faith" since there is no guarantee that publicity will translate into book sales. As famous merchant John Wanamaker said, "Half the money I spend on advertising is wasted; the trouble is I don't know which half."[41] However, it goes without saying, no one ever purchased a book they did not know about. And, a good PR agent can facilitate awareness that can reach far beyond what an author can do on her or his own.

We started this chapter with a sad story; we end with a note of hope. Your best antidote to the "questionable or indifferent" scruples that might be implied by the tone of this chapter is to write a book that emotionally touches all those involved. To paraphrase Melvin Udall (played by Jack Nicholson) in the 1996 hit movie **As Good as it Gets**, your book should make others want to be a better person. Alice Walker wrote: "Writing permits me to be more than I am."[42] Write your book with a spirit that is "big like the ocean, or important like a mountain, or tall like a tree."[43]

Making Your Mark

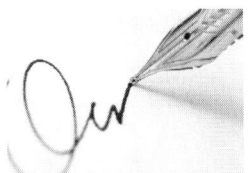

In the early days of our country many people were unable to read or write. Yet, the concept of a signature as a designation of one's acceptance or approval was very much alive and well. You will recall that John Hancock signed the Declaration of Independence with a signature very large so England's King George could read it without his spectacles.

When required to demonstrate their acceptance or approval people were told, "Make your mark." Most signed an "X" to a document. By established law, when a "mark" made by an illiterate signatory was countersigned by a literate witness, it was just as legal as John Hancock's elaborate signature. Being able to "make your mark" consequently became a source of pride.

The phrase "make your mark" today is our common expression for being noticed for a contribution or for the achievement of something impressive. Young people today often hear in graduation speeches: "Go out into the world and make your mark." It is spoken as a message of encouragement for living a life of excellence.

A book is enduring. If you build a house or grow a crop or paint a barn, it will likely become a memory with the artifacts of its existence ultimately eroded with time. But, if a book is copyrighted and given a 13-digit ISBN number, it becomes a part of the collection in the Library of Congress. It is not just cataloged and shelved in its physical form, it is stored in its electronic form. That means your great-great grandchildren will be able to access and read your book. It is a body of work that has your signature mark on its cover. And, it permanently says to the whole universe that you were here and made a contribution. It everlastingly pronounces that you accomplished a worthy achievement.

Let your book mark be one that represents the very best of who you are. Let it reveal your character through the purity of your words, the merit of your themes, and the distinction of your composition. Make it one that touches the lives of all who open its pages to join your characters and concepts on the playground of imagination.

Resources for Writers

Books for Writers

Bell, James Scott, **Plot and Structure: Techniques and Exercises for Crafting a Plot That Grips Readers from Start to Finish 5th Edition** (Cincinnati, OH: Writer's Digest, 2004).

Bradbury, Ray, **Zen in the Art of Writing** (Santa Barbara, CA: Joshua Odell Editions, 1990).

Cameron, Julia, **The Artist Way: A Spiritual Path to Higher Creativity** (New York: Penguin Group, 1992).

Goldbert, Natalie, **Writing Down the Bones: Freeing the Writer Within** (Boulder, CO: Shambhala Publications, 1986).

Grahl, Tim, **Your First 1000 Copies: The Step-by-Step Guide to Marketing Your Book** (Lynchburg, VA: Out:think Group, 2012).

Hall, Tanya, **Ideas, Influence and Income** (Austin, TX: Greenleaf Book Group, 2018).

Hambleton, Vicki and Cathleen Greenwood, **So, You Want to Be a Writer?** (New York: Aladdin, 2012).

Kawasaki, Guy and Shawn Welch, **APE: How to Publish a Book** (New York: Nononini Press, 2013).

King, Stephen, **On Writing: A Memoir of The Craft** (New York: Scribner, 2000).

Kirsh, Jonathan, **Kirsch's Handbook of Publishing Law for Authors, Publishers, Editors and Agents** (Venice, CA: Acrobat Books, 1994).

Lamott, Anne, **Bird by Bird: Instructions on Writing and Life** (New York: Pantheon Books, 1994).

Maass, Donald, **The Emotional Craft of Fiction** (Cincinnati, OH: Writer's Digest Books, 2016).

Mailer, Norman, **The Spooky Art: Thoughts on Writing** (New York: Random House, 2004).

Maran, Meredith, **Why We Write** (New York: Penguin Group, 2013).

McPhee, John, **Draft No. 4: On the Writing Process** (New York: Farrar, Straus & Giroux, 2017).

Penn, Joanna, **Successful Self-Publishing: How to Self-Publish and Market Your Book** (Bath, UK: Curl Up Press, 2018).

Phillip, Larry W. and Mary Welsh Hemingway, **Ernest Hemingway On Writing** (New York: Touchstone, 1984).

Sedwick, Helen, **Self-Publisher's Legal Handbook, 2nd Edition** (Santa Rosa, CA: Ten Gallon Press, 2017).

Singleton, George, **Pep Talks, Warnings, and Screeds: Indispensable Wisdom and Cautionary Advice for Writers** (Cincinnati, OH: Writer's Digest Books, 2008).

Strunk, William and E.B. White, **The Elements of Style, 4th Edition** (London: Pearson Education, LTD., 2013).

Truss, Lynne, **Eats, Shoots and Leaves: The Zero Tolerance Approach to Punctuation** (New York: Penguin Group, 2003).

Weiland, K.M., **Structuring Your Novel** (Barnsley, UK: Pen for A Sword Publishing, 2013).

Zinsser, William, **On Writing Well** (New York: Harper Collins, 2006).

Blog Sites for Writers

Authorsguild.org

EveryWriter.com

Copyblogger.com

AnnKroeker.com

FictionUniversity.com (Fiction)

InkyGirl.com (Children's Books)

Bang2Write.com (Screen Writing)

PositiveWriter.com

CreativIndie.com

Re:Fiction.com (Fiction)

TweetspeakPoetry (Poetry)

Writerology.com

GrammerGirl.com (Editing)

WriterUnboxed.com (Fiction)

Scribendi.com (Editing)

ElnaCain.com (Freelance Writing)

WritersWeekly.com (Freelance Writing)

HubSpot.com (Book Marketing)

MarketingProfs.com (Book Marketing)

SelfPublishingFormula.com (Self-Publishing)

Writer2.0.com

JaneFriedman.com

NovelPublicity.com (Business of Writing)

Standoutbooks.com (Marketing)

TheBookDesigner.com (Book Design)

Chronicles.com (Science Fiction)

Prose.com

SheWrites.com

Bookbutchers.com (Editing)

Talentville.com (Screenwriters)

TheCreativePenn.com

Predatorjournals.com

Writingclasses.com

Support Groups for Authors

Absolutewrite.com

Authonomy.com

Backspace (bksp.org)

Critters.org (science fiction)

Writerschatroom.com

Mywriterscircle.com

National Novel Writing Month (Nanowrimo.org)

Kidlit.com (Children's books)

Querytracker.net (agents)

Fundsforwriters.com

LiteraryFestival.org

ABookInside.blogspot.com

Winningwriters.com (Poetry)

SFWA.org (Science Fiction)

MysteryWriters.org

Romancedivas.com

Poetryoutloud.org

Christianstoryteller.com

Romance Writers of America (Rwanational.org)

Script-o-rama.com

Decaturbookfestival.com

GeorgiaCenterforthebook.org

About the Georgia Writers Museum

Literary works scaffolded the dream that became America. The founding fathers declared independence by signing a *written* document proclaiming their intent. The Constitution set the country on a course to become a nation of *written* laws. Dr. Martin Luther King, Jr. delivered his *written* speech from the steps of the Lincoln Memorial in 1965, dramatically reminding a divided America of its promise of equality.

Literary writings shaped the culture of this great country. At one time, every school child could complete the lines, "I pledge...," "Ask not...," "Four score...," "Oh, say...," "We, the people...," and "I have a...," all familiar sounds from literary creations heralding significant times in our history.

Even as technology transforms how we are entertained, the written word retains a key role in our leisure time and personal development. Books, in either physical, digital or audio form, continue to be in great demand; our news information is shaped by teleprompted scripts, articles, blogs, and columns – all products of the writing process. We still use literacy as a key metric to gauge our advancement as a civilization.

The Georgia Writers Museum celebrates distinction in literary work beginning with three world famous writers —- Alice Walker, Joel Chandler Harris and Flannery O'Conner —- who began their life's journey within miles of the museum. Other Georgia writers are featured through a permanent display of the members of the Georgia Writers Hall of Fame. Still others, less widely known, are featured through book signings and seminars.

Equally important, Georgia Writers Museum incubates the dreams of aspiring writers from school age through retirement age by offering workshops, lectures, and sponsored events, giving all access to and enjoyment of participation in the art of literary expression. It is a resource center for writers and writing enthusiasts. Its goal is to become the literary center of the State.

This goal has been joined by partners in local education, business and visual and performing arts who share the vision to create a new arts destination in Georgia's Lake Country, as a gift to our children, our visitors and art lovers everywhere.

Georgia Writer's Museum
109 S Jefferson Avenue
Eatonton, GA 31024
(706) 991-5119
www.georgiawritersmuseum.com

Use Your Mobile QR Reader to Click on the
QR Code Below to Go Straight to the Website:

About the Contributors
(Listed Alphabetically)

Chip R. Bell

Chip R. Bell is the author of several national best-selling books, including **Take Their Breath Away**, **Managing Knock Your Socks Off Service**, **The 9½ Principles of Innovative Service**, **Magnetic Service**, **Customers as Partners**, **Wired and Dangerous**, **Sprinkles** and his newest book, **Kaleidoscope**. His books have won major book awards, including the 2017 Best Book Award, a 2017 Silver Medal Award from the North American Book Awards, a 2015 GoldInk Award, a 2012 Axiom Book Award, a 2012 IPPY Book award, and a 2004 Benjamin Franklin Book Award. His books have been translated into over a dozen languages. Dr. Bell has appeared live on CNBC, Bloomberg TV, CNN, ABC, CBS, and Fox Business and his work has been featured in *Fortune*, *Wall Street Journal*, *Forbes*, *USA Today*, *Businessweek*, *Entrepreneur, Inc. Magazine, Money Magazine,* and *Fast Company*. A member of the Georgia Writers Museum board, he lives on Lake Oconee, Georgia.

John P. Dennis

John P. Dennis is the author of the Amazon #1 Bestseller, **Men Raised by Women: What He Won't Tell Mom**. John speaks at national conferences as an authority on Single Parenting and Blended Family issues. Audiences have labeled him The Single Mom's Coach, The Step-Dad's Confidant and The Male Mentorship Guru. He is the President of the Georgia Writers Museum & Georgia Writers Hall of Fame. He sits on the Board of Directors for African American Author Literary Awareness Campaign (AAALAC) and also the Board of Directors for Lake Country Arts. John is a veteran of the USAF and owner of NSIGHT TMC.

Mark Engel

Mark Engel spent most of his 44-year journalism career in television news as a reporter and producer at various stations in the Southeastern U.S. He was the News and Local Programming Director at WSB-TV in Atlanta, during which time he ran the station's 100-person news department and guided another department that created locally produced documentaries and specials. He has been honored with the George Foster Peabody Award, 13 regional Emmy Awards and other journalistic recognitions. Mark retired in 2013 following 12 years at CNN as one of a few people authorized to review, revise and approve scripts and stories from correspondents around the world for all CNN platforms. While at CNN, he also trained more than 250 staff members in TV journalism workshops that he created. Mark now lives in Greensboro, Georgia, where he does freelance reporting for the local newspaper and is an FAA licensed drone pilot.

Alice Friman

Alice Friman's sixth full-length collection of poetry is **The View from Saturn** (LSU Press). Her previous book, **Vinculum**, (LSU Press) won the 2012 Georgia Author of the Year Award in Poetry. She is a recipient of a 2012 Pushcart Prize and is included in **Best American Poetry 2009**. Other books include **Inverted Fire** and **The Book of the Rotten Daughter** (both from BkMk Press) and **Zoo** (U. of Arkansas Press) which won the Sheila Margaret Motton Prize from The New England Poetry Club and the Ezra Pound Poetry Award from Truman State University. Her work has appeared in *Poetry, The Georgia Review, The Gettysburg Review, The Southern Review, Shenandoah,* and many others. Professor emerita of English and creative writing at the University of Indianapolis, she now lives in Milledgeville, Georgia, where she was Poet-in-Residence at Georgia College.

George Heiring

George's short stories, essays and poems are featured in seven books and fifteen literary and poetry anthologies. He is the author of two regional best sellers, **The Seasonal Heart** and **Turning Leaves** and a children's book, **I Will Stay with You.** His musical comedy "30" has been staged in community theaters in several Midwestern cities. His recent literary honors include the Byron Herbert Reece International Award, the Anderson Social Poetry Prize, and the Founders and Mnemosyne Awards.

George currently serves as the interim President of the Georgia Writers Museum in Eatonton, Georgia. His business career was largely focused on advising major corporations on employee communication. George and his wife, Donna, live on the shores of Lake Oconee in central Georgia.

Terry Kay

A 2009 recipient of the Governor's Award in the Humanities and a 2006 inductee into the Georgia Writers Hall of Fame, Terry Kay is the author of seventeen books, including the recently released **The King Who Made Paper Flowers**. Other books include **The Book of Marie, Taking Lottie Home, The Kidnapping of Aaron Greene, Shadow Song, Dark Thirty, After Eli,** and **To Whom the Angel Spoke.** Three of his novels have been produced as Hallmark Hall of Fame movies, **To Dance with the White Dog, The Runaway,** and **The Valley of Light**. His books have been published in more than twenty foreign languages, with **To Dance with the White Dog** selling two million copies in Japan. In 2011, Kay was presented the Lifetime Achievement Award by the Georgia Writers Association. He has received the Georgia Author of the Year award four times and in 2004 was presented with the Townsend Prize, considered the state›s top literary award. Kay and his wife reside in Athens, GA.

Lisa Earle McLeod

Lisa Earle McLeod is a global thought leader in purpose-driven business. Her first book, **Forget Perfect**, launched the movement to help women find more purpose and happiness. Her national bestseller, **Selling with Noble Purpose**, introduced Noble Purpose into the business vernacular. Her newest book, **Leading with Noble Purpose: How to Create a Tribe of True Believers** has been called a breakthrough book that is transforming the way businesses are lead. A former Procter & Gamble sales trainer, she now runs her own consulting firm, McLeod & More, Inc. Her firm's clients include Hootsuite, Roche, and Dave & Busters. She is a prolific writer with over 2,000 articles. She is the sales leadership expert for Forbes.com and has appeared on *Oprah*, the *Today Show* and the *NBC Nightly News*. Lisa lives on Lake Oconee GA with her husband, Bob.

Derin Moore, CMC

Chef Derin Moore is the Executive Chef for Reynolds Lake Oconee. Prior to coming to Reynolds, he enjoyed a diverse career including fine dining, platinum country clubs, and most recently the executive chef at the Ritz Carlton Hotel in Naples, Florida, where he maintained Mobile Five Star and AAA Diamond status for four seasons. He has a Masters in Cookery from the world-renowned CFEI/Culinary Institute of America and is one of only 72 Certified Master Chefs in the USA. He has received over 30 industry honors nationally and internationally for for his many accomplishments in the culinary industry. He was a team member for ACF Culinary Team USA from 1992 to 2000, garnering more than 20 international gold medals. He has also served as an adjunct professor at a number of recognized culinary colleges. Chef Derin lives on Lake Oconee.

Gail Vail

Gail Vail has been an avid painter and writer for most of her life. Born in Nebraska, she earned a B.A. in Business and pursued a career in marketing and human resources with IBM. Her career ultimately brought her, husband Hugh, and children to Atlanta. Raising a family, combined with a professional career, sidetracked her love of painting and writing for a time. Now retired, she has again picked up her pen and her brush, becoming a prolific painter. Her first published book, **Seasons on Lake Oconee**, includes writings and paintings by forty area authors and artists. Her second and third published books, **The Seasonal Heart** and **Turning Leaves**, are collaborations with area author George Heiring. Her paintings are included in six published books. She also enjoys public speaking, especially relating how faith and patience have played a role in book publishing.

Acknowledgements

We have many people to thank for their help in making this book possible:

Georgia Writers Museum, especially museum president John P. Dennis, interim president George Heiring, board members Paula Benjamin, Shelagh Fagan, Janet Kelhoffer, Jack Shinneman, and executive director Vickie Spivey,

Ray Bard, CEO of Bard Books, Austin, Texas, for advice on Chapter 15,

Justin Branch, Acquisitions Editor for Greenleaf Book Group, Austin, Texas, for advice on Chapter 15,

Leslie Stephen in Austin, Texas, for her developmental editing work,

Jamey Fuller in El Paso, Texas, for her copyediting work,

Kristine R. Moore Tarrer, attorney-at-law and Lake Country Arts board member, for help with copyright application,

Adam Soffer, attorney-at-law, Soffer-Charbonnet, Minneapolis, Minnesota, for advice on Chapter 18,

Becky Robinson, CEO of Weaving Influence, Lambertville, Michigan, for her advice on Chapter 16,

Drs. Patty and Jack Phillips of ROI Institute in Birmingham, Alabama, for advice on Chapter 2,

Kathy Wright and Susan Erlandson for help identifying potential contributors,

Linda Foster, vice president of the Artisan's Village Guild, for help selecting a cover artist,

Lou Benjamin, president of Lake Country Arts,

Eric Arena, superintendent of Putnam County Schools, Eatonton, GA, and

Gail Vail, local popular artist, for the cover art.

Endnotes and References

1. Lyrics by Joe Raposo, "Being Green," 1970, featured in **The Muppet Movie** directed by Jim Henson, used with written permission from the Disney Music Publishing.
2. Ernest Hemingway, **Ernest Hemingway on Writing**, by Larry W. Phillip and Mary Welsh Hemingway, New York: Touchstone, 1984, p. 29.
3. Samuel L. Clemens (Mark Twain), **The Adventures of Tom Sawyer**, New York: Dover Publications, 1998.
4. Henry Martin, *The New Yorker*, 1980, Reprinted with permission from the Tribune Company Syndicate, Inc.
5. William Shakespeare, **Henry V**, Act 1, Prologue.
6. Samuel Taylor Coleridge, 1772-1834, No source identified.
7. Annie Dillard, **The Writing Life**, New York: Harper & Row, 1989, p. 78.
8. Maya Angelou, *The Paris Review*, Fall, 1990, a transcript of an interview with George Plimpton held at the YMHA in Manhattan in 1990.
9. Hemingway, **Ernest Hemingway On Writing**, p. 41.
10. Annie Dillard, **The Writing Life**, p.75.
11. Phil Pullman, "Questions and Answers" on www.phillip-pullman.com, March 9, 2009.
12. Venus Williams, **Come to Win**, New York: HarperCollins, 2010, p. xvii.

13. John Steinbeck, Conversation with George Plimpton and first reported in Pen America 4: Fact/Fiction (www.pen.org).
14. Orson Scott Card, "A Conversation with Orson Scott Card," by Claire E. White, *The Internet Writing Journal*, September, 1999 (www. writerswrite.com).
15. Ernest Hemingway, **Ernest Hemingway on Writing**, p. 37.
16. Benjamin Disraeli, Speech at banquet given by the city of Glasgow for Disraeli on his inauguration as Lord Rector of Glasgow University (19 November 1870), cited in **Wit and Wisdom of Benjamin Disraeli, Collected from His Writings and Speeches** (1881), p. 16.
17. Norman Mailer, **The Spooky Art: Thoughts on Writing**, New York: Random House, 2004, p. 88.
18. Interview with Terry Kay by Chip R. Bell, January 10, 2018.
19. **The Magic of Belle Isle**, written by Guy Thomas, released in 2012 by Castle Rock Entertainment.
20. Susan Sontag, At the Same Time: Essays and Speeches, New York: Farrar, Straus and Giroux, 2007, p. 143.
21. Annie Dillard, **The Writing Life**, p. 7.
22. Kurt Vonnegut, "Dear Mr. Vonnegut," *In These Times*, February 28, 2003.
23. William Zinsser, **On Writing Well**, New York: Harper Collins, 2006, p. 297.
24. George Singleton, **Pep Talks, Warnings, and Screeds: Indispensable Wisdom and Cautionary Advice for Writers**, Cincinnati, OH: Writer's Digest Books, 2008, p. 59.
25. Henry David Thoreau, **The Journey 1837-1861**, New York: NY Review of Books Classic, 2009, p. 293.
26. Ernest Hemingway, quote from *NY Journal-American* (July 11, 1961).
27. Ernest Hemingway, "Monologue to the Maestro," *Esquire Magazine*, October 1935, p. 21.
28. Truman Capote, quote from an interview on PBS *The Dick Cavett Show*, 1980.
29. Truss, Lynne, **Eats, Shoots and Leaves: The Zero Tolerance Approach to Punctuation** (New York: Penguin Group, 2003).

30. Grisham, John, "John Grisham's Suggestions for Writing Popular Fiction," *NY Times Book Review*, June 4, 2017, p. BR31.

31. Hare, Anne, "Writing Life Stories for the Inspirational or Religious Markets," *The Internet Writing Journal, September 1999.*

32. Steven Piersanti, "The 10 Awful Truths about Book Publishing," www.bkconnection.com, Updated September 26, 2016.

33. Ralph Waldo Emerson, quoted in *Oakland Daily Evening Tribune (Oakland Tribune)*, May 20, 1882, p. 2, Col. 1.

34. Tara Hunt, **The Whuffie Factor**, New York: Crown Books, 2009, p. 4.

35. H.G. Wells, *H. G. Wells: A Biography,* by Norman and Jeanne Mackenzie, New York: *Simon & Schuster. p. 333.*

36. **Ratatouille**, motion picture produced by Pixar, 2007, based on original story written by Jan Pinkava, Jim Capobianco and Brad Bird.

37. **Forrest Gump,** motion picture produced by Paramount Pictures, 1984, based original novel by Winston Groom. The line, "Life is like a box of chocolates..." was derived from the book **Norwegian Wood** by Haruki Murakami.

38. "'Gump,' a Huge Hit, Still Isn't Raking in Huge Profits? Hmm," by Bernard Weinraub, *NY Times*, May 25, 1995.

39. "What Accounting Lesson Winston Groom Learned from the Movie Forrest Gump," Konvexity.wordpress.com (CFA Level I. CFA Level 11, January 12, 2013).

40. Jean Shepard, **In God We Trust: All Others Pay Cash**, New York: Doubleday Books, 1966.

41. John Wanamaker, **John Wanamaker: King of Merchants**, by William Allen Zulker, Wayne, PA: Eaglecrest Press, 1993, p. 77.

42. Alice Walker, **The World Has Changed: Conversations with Alice Walker,** by Rudolph P. Byrd, New York: The New Press, 2010, p. 54.

43. Lyrics by Joe Raposo, "Being Green," 1970, featured in **The Muppet Movie** directed by Jim Henson, used with written permission from the Disney Music Publishing.